CRAFTS FOR CREATIVE WORSHIP

Jan Brind is a wife, mother and pastoral musician. She is a member of the Diocesan Worship Committee in Guildford, and a pastoral Assisant at St Andrew's Church, Cobham. She helps run workshops and facilitate music days which encourage parishes to use new songs and be creative with liturgy.

Tessa Wilkinson is is a wife, mother, grandmother, artist and counsellor. She passionately believes that everyone can be, and should be, creative. Over the years she has lived and worked in many different parishes and enjoyed encouraging others to discover their creative gifts. She now lives in London.

CREATIVE WORKSHOPS

Jan and Tessa are available to run creative workshops for festivals and seasons. For parish or deanery groups, ministerial or lay training groups, and theological colleges, workshops include songs, candle decoration, bags for life, and design ideas for banners and altar frontals – all held within a structure of worship and fun. For more information please contact them at jandtworkshops@hotmail.com

CRAFTS FOR CREATIVE WORSHIP

A resource and activity book for parishes

Jan Brind and Tessa Wilkinson

CANTERBURY
PRESS
Norwich

© Jan Brind and Tessa Wilkinson 2004, 2009

First published in 2004 by the Canterbury Press Norwich
Editorial office
13–17 Long Lane,
London, EC1A 9PN, UK

Second edition published in 2009

Canterbury Press is an imprint of Hymns Ancient and Modern Ltd
(a registered charity)
St Mary's Works, St Mary's Plain,
Norwich, NR3 3BH, UK

www.scm-canterburypress.co.uk

British Library Cataloguing in Publication data

A catalogue record for this book is available
from the British Library

978 1 84825 004 8

Printed and bound in Great Britain by
CPI Antony Rowe, Chippenham SN14 6LH

Dedication

This book is dedicated to our husbands, children and grandchildren

Robin
Sophie, Anna and Dave
Guy
Hugh, Lizzie, Eli, Ruth, Martha and Dorie
John, Beccy and Molly
Thomas, Lucy and Alexander

With grateful thanks to the Christian communities who have allowed us to be creative with liturgy

Holy Cross Church, Coventry
All Saints' Church, Ockham
All Saints' Church, Small Heath
St Columba's House, Woking
St Andrew's Church, Cobham
St Peter's Church, Wolvercote, Oxford

CONTENTS

Readings for Advent · Hymns and Songs for Advent · Advent Hymn · Prayers for Advent · An Advent Prayer · Christmas Carol Services During Advent · Banners Using Words from Advent Sunday Readings · Banners and Altar Frontals for Advent · Banners Using the Fig Tree · Altar Frontals or Wall Hangings Using Pockets · Advent Rings · Designs for Advent Stoles · Advent Cards · Advent Calendars · The Jesse Tree · Parish Activities for Advent · Pew Sheet Puzzles · Are You Ready for Christmas?

Readings for Christmas Day · Hymns and Songs for Christmas · Children's Nativity Song · Christmas Hymn · Prayers for Christmas Day · Long Hanging Christmas Banners · Banners, Frontals and Stoles Using the Good News · Mosaic Banner · Patchwork Banner · Banners Using 'The

EASTER   123

ORDINARY TIME   173

HOW TO . . .   215

IN THE LIGHT OF THE LORD

Advent brings firelight
Snow-light and twilight
Calendars, candlelight
Carols and angel light

Christmas brings holy light
Stable-light, manger-light
Child in his mother's arms
Swaddled in Christ Light

Shepherds are watching
Their sheep in the moonlight
Chosen to worship
The child in the limelight

Epiphany, and wise men
Follow the star-light
Gold, myrrh and frankincense
Gifts for the Promised Light

Rainbows in Lenten-light
Gathering storm-light
Soldiers and lantern light
Betrayal and no light

Easter brings Paschal Light
Forgiveness and new life
The Cross is triumphant
And Christ is the True Light

Summer brings Pentecost
Power, wind and flame-light
Spirit and dove-light
Love, joy and peace-light

Autumn and sun-light
Red, orange, gold light
The earth in full circle
Waits quietly for New Light

Introduction

The different seasons in the church calendar give us wonderful opportunities to be creative and to try something new. A church that is alive to change, and where people engage in experiment, can become a church more fully alive. In this book you will find ideas and suggestions to help your church community celebrate Feast Days and Seasons. In each section you will find readings (either the set readings from the Revised Common Lectionary or other readings relevant to the theme), suggested hymns and songs, prayers, ideas for instant artwork to decorate your church building, and ideas for parish activities to draw people together. We have followed the main seasons in the church calendar. We hope that the emphasis given is one of looking 'outwards' rather than 'inwards'. Many of the suggested activities invite us to look beyond our parish or church boundaries in order to show the love of God in the wider world.

The Bible passages quoted are taken from the New International Version and the Good News Bible.

How to Use this Book

The artwork resources and ideas for activities in this book can be used in a number of ways. Your church may have an inspired and creative worship team and you may already be accustomed to transforming your worship space with instant banners, altar frontals and vestments, and your worship with creative ideas. In this case you can use this book as a 'pick and mix' selection – it may give you some new thoughts or a fresh approach to something already tried. For others, the ideas in this book may be entirely new. They may be just the things you need to inspire a flagging spirit or a diminishing congregation! Gather a small group of people together, choose something simple, introduce it gently to your church congregation and see what happens! Or be brave and transform the inside of your church, and your worship, almost overnight. You may be surprised at the result and, indeed, the reaction! Remember, though, that a lot of people find the idea of change difficult and threatening – so be mindful of that. You know your own congregation better than anyone.

Organizing and running a workshop is an excellent way of preparing a church for the celebration of a festival and, in the next chapter, there is an outline plan of how to do this.

Many of the suggested hymns and songs listed at the beginning of each chapter are deliberately chosen because they may be less well-known. There is a wealth of available hymnody just waiting to be discovered and enjoyed, including much by contemporary composers. The authors make no apology for crossing the ecumenical boundaries! Music in our worship is so important and it is well worth thinking carefully about your choice of hymns and songs. We tend to become reliant on the familiar material given in our pew hymnbooks. By buying just one copy of one or two new hymnbooks you will have so much more to draw on. You can print the words to a new song on your parish pew sheet and teach them to the congregation. Just make sure your copyright licence is up to date. For many of the songs we suggest you will need both a Christian Copyright Licence and a Calamus Licence. A Calamus Licence covers many of the songs from the Roman Catholic Church and also music from Taizé and is available from Decani Music. Many new songs fit to well-established and familiar tunes – this makes it an easy and non-threatening way to introduce new material. If you introduce a new song firmly believing in people's ability to sing it you will find that they do! Look at the given list of hymnbooks and publishers. This is obviously not exhaustive – and is being added to all the time – and, of course, the hymns and songs chosen are taken from our own collection of hymnbooks and are our own choices. You may want to choose others. Also, please note that many of the suggested songs are in more than one hymnbook but are only listed once.

The final section in the book will give you instructions for making a lot of the things that are mentioned. The book is aiming to encourage people to try new things and, above all, to be creative, so we have tried to keep instructions very simple. Have fun!

We are very pleased that this new edition has an accompanying CD. Please use it to download and print off anything you need to reproduce where, in the first edition, we suggested photocopying. Please feel free to change or adapt the material to make it appropriate to your particular situation. We do ask, though, that you acknowledge our copyright on words and artwork that are ours.

The Resource Cupboard

Being creative is greatly helped by having at least a few resources on hand and available in a Parish Resource Cupboard. Below are three lists. The first list is of essential materials and items that it would be good to have on hand all the time. The second list gives more specialist materials and items that can be collected over time, or as and when they are needed. Finally, there is a 'wish' list of items that it would be fun to have but which are not essential. Following these there are suggested lists of people and places to put on a possible database. This information might be helpful when planning a parish event and enable planners to source people and materials quickly.

Try to be organized with resources. Keeping things in well-marked boxes will enable anyone to access the materials or items easily and return them for future use. Collect shoe boxes, plastic boxes and ice cream tubs. Mark the contents clearly with a marker pen.

List of essential materials and items

Brown parcel tape
Butterfly clips
Cocktail sticks
Coloured card
Coloured paper
Craft knives
Crayons
Double-sided sticky
   tape
Drawing pins
Dressing up clothes for
   drama
Erasers
Extension cable
Fabric

Fabric paints
Felt pens
   Fabric markers
   Permanent markers
   Thick and thin
      markers
   Washable markers
Floor covering
Glitter
Glue
   Fabric
   Paper
   PVA
Glue brushes
Hole punch

Iron
Ironing board
Kitchen roll
Lining paper
Magazines
Newspapers
Paintbrushes
Paper
Paper clips
Pencils
Pins and needles
Plastic rubbish bags
Polystyrene food trays
Rags
Ruler

Safety pins
Scissors
Scrap fabric
Scrap paper
Selection of self-
   adhesive spots and
   stars

Sellotape
Spray bottles
Spray glue
Staple gun and staples
Stapler and staples
Stencil brushes
String and thread

Tape measure
Thumb tacks
Tin or aluminium foil
Wallpaper
Wax fabric crayons
Wire

List of specialist materials and items

Aerosol spray paint
Baking trays
Bamboo poles
Baskets
Biscuit cutters
Black paper
Candles
Cardboard candle drip
   guards
Cellophane
Cupcake/bun/muffin
   tins
Diffusers

Dowelling rods
Dried leaves
Electoral roll
Empty plastic bottles
Face masks
Flower pots
Glass relief outliner
Lollypop sticks
Masonry nails
Oasis
Old Christmas cards
Paper cases
Polystyrene balls

Polystyrene plates
Ribbon
Sand
Shoe boxes
Silver and gold pens
Socks – old and clean
Stencils
Stones
Tinsel
Wire rings
Wooden spoons

'Wish' list

Artificial flowers
Atlas
Badge maker
Bubble blowers
Camera
CD player
Collection of adult and
   children's CDs
Computer

Crib figures and
   stable
Display boards
Fabric stiffener
Guillotine
Hot glue gun
Internet access
Laminator
Map of the world

Musical instruments
Photocopier
Plastic eggs
Projector and screen
Sewing machine
Star-shaped cake tin
Useful books
Video camera
White fairy lights

Database of useful people and places

People who can . . .

Act	Direct drama	Sew
Arrange flowers	Garden	Sing
Be creative	Make music	Write prayers
Cook	Organize	

Places where you can acquire . . .

Art and craft materials	Fabric – local mills	Sand and stones
Cake decorations	Flowers	Specialist foods
Candles	Paper – local mills	Stationery
DIY	Recycled material	

Contact names and addresses of, for example . . .

Ambulance stations	Hotels	Nursing and residential
Churches Together reps	Inns and restaurants	homes
Colleges	Local authorities	People with gardens
Dentists	Local industry	Police stations
Fire brigade	Local services	Prisons
Garden centres	Local shops	Schools
GP surgeries	Local small businesses	Traffic wardens
Health centres	Markets with opening	
Hospitals	times	

A Selection of Hymnbooks
and Song Books

Anglican Hymns Old & New, compiled by Kevin Mayhew, Kevin Mayhew, 2008

Be Still and Know, compiled by Margaret Rizza, Kevin Mayhew, 2000

Beneath a Travelling Star, Timothy Dudley-Smith, Canterbury Press, 2001

Cantate, edited by Stephen Dean, Decani Music, 2005

Carol Praise, edited by David Peacock with Noël Tredinnick, Collins, 2006

Celtic Hymn Book, selected by Ray Simpson, Kevin Mayhew, 2005

Christ, Be Our Light, Bernadette Farrell, OCP Publications, 1994. (Available from Decani Music)

Come All You People: Shorter songs for worship, John L. Bell, Wild Goose Publications, 1994

Common Ground: A song book for all the churches, John L. Bell and Editorial Committee, Saint Andrew Press, 1994

Common Praise, compiled by Hymns Ancient and Modern Ltd, Canterbury Press, 2000

Complete Anglican Hymns Old & New, compiled by Geoffrey Moore, Susan Sayers, Michael Forster and Kevin Mayhew, Kevin Mayhew, 2000

Drawn to the Wonder: Hymns and songs from churches worldwide, compiled by Francis Brienen and Maggie Hamilton, Council for World Mission, 1995

Enemy of Apathy, John L. Bell and Graham Maule, Wild Goose Publications, 1988 (Revised 1990)

Fire of Love, Margaret Rizza, Kevin Mayhew, 1998

Fountain of Life, Margaret Rizza, Kevin Mayhew, 1997

Gather, edited by Robert J. Batastini, GIA Publications Inc., 1994 (Second edition)

Go Before Us, Bernadette Farrell, OCP Publications, 2003 (Available from Decani Music)

God Beyond All Names, Bernadette Farrell, OCP Publications, 1991 (Available from Decani Music)

Heaven Shall Not Wait, John L. Bell and Graham Maule, Wild Goose Publications, 1987 (Reprinted 1994)

Hymns of Glory, Songs of Praise, editorial panel convened by the Church of Scotland and led by John L. Bell and Charles Robertson, Canterbury Press (on behalf of the Church Hymnary Trust), 2008

Hymns Old and New: New Anglican Edition, compiled by Geoffrey Moore, Susan Sayers, Michael Forster and Kevin Mayhew, Kevin Mayhew, 1996

Hymns Old & New: One Church, One Faith, One Lord, compiled by Colin Mawby, Kevin Mayhew, Susan Sayers, Ray Simpson and Stuart Thomas, Kevin Mayhew, 2004

Innkeepers and Light Sleepers: Songs for Christmas, John L. Bell, Wild Goose Publications, 1992

Iona Abbey Music Book: Songs from the Iona Abbey Worship Book, compiled by the Iona Community, Wild Goose Publications, 2003

Light in Our Darkness, Margaret Rizza, Kevin Mayhew, 2002

Laudate, edited by Stephen Dean, Decani Music, 2000

Liturgical Hymns Old and New, compiled by Robert Kelly, Sister Sheila McGovern SSL, Kevin Mayhew, Father Andrew Moore and Sister Louisa Poole SSL, Kevin Mayhew, 1999

Love and Anger: Songs of lively faith and social justice, John L. Bell and Graham Maule, Wild Goose Publications, 1997

Love from Below, John L. Bell and Graham Maule, Wild Goose Publications, 1989

Many and Great: Songs of the world church, John L. Bell, Wild Goose Publications, 1990

Methodist Hymns Old and New, compiled by Revd Peter Bolt, Revd Amos Cresswell, Mrs Tracy Harding and Revd Ray Short, Kevin Mayhew, 2001

New Start Hymns and Songs, compiled by Kevin Mayhew, Kevin Mayhew, 1999

One Is the Body: Songs of unity and diversity, John L. Bell, Wild Goose Publications, 2002

Restless Is the Heart, Bernadette Farrell, OCP Publications, 2000 (Available from Decani Music)

Resurrexit: Music for Lent, the Easter Triduum and Eastertide, edited by Stephen Dean, Decani Music, 2001

River of Peace, Margaret Rizza, Kevin Mayhew, 1998

Sent by the Lord: Songs of the world church, John L. Bell and Graham Maule, Wild Goose Publications, 1991

Share the Light, Bernadette Farrell, OCP Publications, 2000 (Available from Decani Music)

Sing Glory: Hymns, psalms and songs for a new century, edited by Michael Baughen, Kevin Mayhew, 1999

Songs and Prayers from Taizé, Ateliers et Presses de Taizé, Continuum, 1991

Songs for Prayer, Ateliers et Presses de Taizé, Ateliers et Presses de Taizé, 1998

Songs from Taizé, Ateliers et Presses de Taizé (Published annually)

Songs of Fellowship, compiled by members of Kingsway Music Editorial Team, Kingsway Music, 1991

The Children's Hymnbook, compiled by Kevin Mayhew, Kevin Mayhew, 1997

The Courage to Say No: Songs for Lent and Easter, John L. Bell and Graham Maule, Wild Goose Publications, 1996

There Is One Among Us: Shorter songs for worship, John L. Bell, Wild Goose Publications, 1998

The Source 3, definitive worship collection, compiled by Graham Kendrick, Kevin Mayhew, 2005

Twenty-First Century Folk Hymnal, compiled by Kevin Mayhew, Kevin Mayhew, 1999

Veni Emmanuel: Music for Advent and Christmastide, edited by Stephen Dean, Decani Music, 2001

We Walk His Way, shorter songs for worship, John L. Bell, Wild Goose Publications, 2008

When Grief Is Raw: Songs for times of sorrow and bereavement, John L. Bell and Graham Maule, Wild Goose Publications, 1997

World Praise, David Peacock and Geoff Weaver, Marshall Pickering, 1993

Worship, edited by Robert J. Batastini, GIA Publications Inc., 1986 (Third edition)

WORKSHOPS

Organizing a Workshop

The purpose of a workshop is to bring together a group of people from the church congregation and from the community, of all ages, to prepare themselves and the church building for a festival or event. Advent, Christmas, Lent, Mothering Sunday, Easter, Pentecost, Harvest, Patronal Festivals and Saints Days all lend themselves to this sort of activity.

You may have an obvious group of people who can make up a Workshop Team or you may need to create a special group or 'working party'. A Sunday School or Youth Group with adult leaders would be good. A Mothers and Toddlers group, a Men's Breakfast Fellowship, a Lunch Club or a House Group – all these can form working parties. Your local Church School might enjoy the challenge of preparing the church for, for example, Mothering Sunday. Adult-only groups work well, too. It is surprising how much fun adults can have when let loose with glue and paint and their imagination!

A workshop runs for a couple of hours, usually either on a Saturday morning before a major church festival on the following Sunday, or immediately after the morning service a week or two before a church festival – when people can stay on without too much effort. It is important that this group should have a good time, enjoy each other's company and get to know each other.

What happens at a workshop?

- people are welcomed
- name badges are made
- the theme is explained
- songs are learned
- any whole group activity takes place
- coffee and refreshments are served
- people break into small groups to make things
- people draw together again to look at what has been made

- a meal is shared
- people go home

In church the following day anything that has been prepared at the workshop is put in place, or is carried out, or is performed – songs are sung, prayers are read, plays are acted out.

Planning a workshop

A workshop needs to be well-planned in advance. A group of at least six people are needed for initial planning well ahead of the event – more is great, any less and the work is much harder!

Workshop Planning Meeting

AGENDA

1 **Festival** and **theme** of the workshop.
2 **Date** of the workshop.
   This is usually planned for the Saturday morning before a festival on the following Sunday *or* immediately after a morning service.
3 **Time** of the workshop.
4 **Venue** of the workshop – book if necessary.
5 **Activities** to take place which fit the theme of the workshop – one at least of which can be a 'whole group' activity and several of which should be 'small group' activities. Brainstorming ideas can include any of the following:
   • banner making
   • altar frontal making
   • vestment making (stole, chasuble)
   • singing a new song
   • cooking
   • rehearsing a play
   • flower arranging
   • making something (cards, models)
   • finding something (treasure hunt)
   • a quiz
   • a whole group activity
   • a prayer group to plan intercessions
   • a reading group to look at the set readings
6 Decide who will run each group and what will be needed.

7   Plan what will happen as people start to arrive – name badges.

8   Plan and decide who will bring food for the refreshments and shared meal. The meal can be simple, comprising soup, sandwiches, crisps, sausage rolls and cake, with hot and cold drinks. If everyone in the planning group brings one thing there is no need for a major effort on any one person's part.

9   Discuss who will be invited.

10   Decide who will send out invitations and look after publicity.

Things to remember when planning activities

It is important to remember that this is a workshop for all ages, so some groups may be for adults only, some for children only and some for both age groups working together.

It is also really important to remember those in the church building who are cleaning the church, arranging the flowers, cleaning the brass and generally preparing the building for Sunday. They can be asked to come and join the workshop group at the beginning, especially if there is a song to be learned, at coffee and refreshment time, and for the shared meal at the end.

And finally . . .

Stress to everyone who is involved in the running of the workshop how important it is to be at the venue in good time (at least half an hour before) to get everything ready before the participants arrive!

ADVENT

The first season of the liturgical year is Advent. It is a time of preparation, both practically in terms of getting ready for the Christmas festivities, but also spiritually as we prepare ourselves to welcome Jesus into our lives. Because Advent is all about 'getting ready' and 'being prepared' it seems an excellent season for making the church 'ready'. But it can often be a season that gets skipped over because people are looking ahead to Christmas.

It is worth noting that most of the readings concern our readiness, or not, for the Second Coming. It is only the last Sunday of Advent that speaks of the nativity of Jesus.

In this part we give suggestions for reconciling themes of Advent with Christmas carol services. We give strong emphasis to church decorations that speak of 'being ready' and 'being alert' for the Second Coming of Christ. We give various ideas for making Advent calendars either as part of the church decoration or individually to give away. We look at a Jesse Tree that can be used as a symbolic focus up to and including The Presentation of Christ in the Temple. Activities focus very much on looking beyond the parish to the wider community and include suggestions for practical gift-giving to those in need. There is also a simple play to perform.

READINGS FOR ADVENT

Advent Sunday

A Isaiah 2.1–5
   Psalm 122
   Romans 13.11–14
   Matthew 24.36–44
B Isaiah 64.1–9
   Psalm 80.1–8, 18–20
   1 Corinthians 1.3–9
   Mark 13.24–37
C Jeremiah 33.14–16
   Psalm 25.1–9
   1 Thessalonians 3.9–13
   Luke 21.25–36

Second Sunday in Advent

A Isaiah 11.1–10
   Psalm 72.1–7, 18–19
   Romans 15.4–13
   Matthew 3.1–12
B Isaiah 40.1–11
   Psalm 85.1–2, 8–13
   2 Peter 3.8–15a
   Mark 1.1–8
C Baruch 5.1–9
   or Malachi 3.1–4
   Canticle Benedictus
   Philippians 1.3–11
   Luke 3.1–6

Third Sunday in Advent

A Isaiah 35.1–10
   Psalm 146.4–10 *or* Canticle Magnificat
   James 5.7–10
   Matthew 11.2–11
B Isaiah 61.1–4, 8–11
   Psalm 126 *or* Canticle Magnificat
   1 Thessalonians 5.16–24
   John 1.6–8, 19–28
C Zephaniah 3.14–20
   Canticle Isaiah 12.2–6
   Philippians 4.4–7
   Luke 3.7–18

Fourth Sunday in Advent

A Isaiah 7.10–16
   Psalm 80.1–8, 18–20
   Romans 1.1–7
   Matthew 1.18–25
B 2 Samuel 7.1–11, 16
   Canticle Magnificat *or* Psalm 89.1–4, 19–26
   Romans 16.25–27
   Luke 1.26–38
C Micah 5.2–5a
   Canticle Magnificat *or* Psalm 80.1–8
   Hebrews 10.5–10
   Luke 1.39–45 (46–55)

HYMNS AND SONGS FOR ADVENT

Details of these hymn books and song books are on pages xxi–xxiv.

Carol Praise

My Lord, he is a-coming soon

Fountain of Life

Come, Lord
Magnificat

Go Before Us

We are waiting

Heaven Shall Not Wait

Cloth for the cradle

Hymns of Glory, Songs of Praise

Come now, O Prince of peace
Comfort, comfort now my people
Hope is a candle, once lit by the prophets
Lift up your heads, eternal gates
People, look East. The time is near
Sound the trumpet, the Lord is near

Hymns Old and New: New Anglican Edition

For Mary, mother of our Lord
From heaven you came
God's Spirit is in my heart

Innkeepers and Light Sleepers

Carol of the Advent
Christmas is coming
No wind at the window

Laudate

Benedictus
Come to set us free
Litany of the Word
Now bless the God of Israel

Songs and Prayers from Taizé

Come and fill our hearts with your peace (Confitemini Domino)
In the Lord
Wait for the Lord

Veni Emmanuel

Advent lullaby
Blest be the God of Israel
He came down that we may have love
He comes to us as one unknown
O child of promise, come
Prepare the way of the Lord

ADVENT HYMN

Tune: Westminster Abbey 87 87 87

1 Light a candle for God's people,
   gathered here in joyful throng;
   love embrace both friend and stranger,
   as we raise our Advent song.
   Shine the light for all God's people;
   let it shine for all to see!

2 Light a candle for the prophets,
   given wondrous news to tell;
   'One will come to light the darkness,
   God with us, Emmanuel!'
   Shine the light for all the prophets;
   let it shine for all to see!

3 Light a candle for the Baptist,
   making sure the path is clear;
   'Be prepared to greet the Saviour,
   for his time is ever near.'
   Shine the light for John the Baptist;
   let it shine for all to see!

4 Light a candle for the Virgin,
   soon to bear the infant King;
   chosen, blessed above all others,
   praises now to her we sing.
   Shine the light for Virgin Mary;
   let it shine for all to see!

5   Light a candle for the Christ child,
      now the promise is fulfilled;
      Prince of Peace, and hope of nations,
      in an infant is revealed.
      Shine the brightest light for Jesus;
      let it shine for all to see!

© Jan Brind

PRAYERS FOR ADVENT

Intercessions

Let us offer prayers to God, our heavenly Father:
You sent your Son Jesus to live among us and bring good news to the oppressed.
May we provide shelter for the homeless and a place of safety for the refugee and asylum seeker. May we find ways to cut across barriers of race and religion to welcome strangers into our hearts and lives. We pray that justice and peace might rule in the hearts of all people.
Hear us, good Lord,
And may your kingdom come, here on earth.

You sent your Son Jesus to heal the broken-hearted.
We pray for people in broken relationships, for single parents and for orphaned children. We pray for the lonely and lost and for those who feel abandoned and let down by society. May we bring comfort and support to those in need and find a better way of caring for each other.
Hear us, good Lord,
And may your kingdom come, here on earth.

You sent your Son Jesus to free the prisoner.
We pray for all who suffer from any kind of addiction or dependency. May they find the right means of support to overcome their illness and trust in you that all will be well. Help us to be a people who do not judge, but who reach out to those in need.
Hear us, good Lord,
And may your kingdom come, here on earth.

You sent your Son Jesus to proclaim the year of the Lord's favour.
At this jubilee time may we have the grace to give and receive forgiveness for past wrongs. We pray for peace in your world. May this Advent be a time of new beginnings when debts can be cancelled and relationships can be healed.
Hear us, good Lord,
And may your kingdom come, here on earth.

You sent your Son Jesus to comfort all who mourn.
We pray for people who are bereaved. We pray that we may know how to listen and to find gentle ways of helping them in their sorrow. We pray for the unemployed and those suffering any kind of loss. May we reassure them of their worth and offer them support.
Hear us, good Lord,
And may your kingdom come, here on earth.

AN ADVENT PRAYER

God of the sun and the moon and the stars and of all the powers of heaven, you sent your Son Jesus Christ to bring the good news of joy and mercy and righteousness to humankind. We pray that we may find ourselves awake, prepared and ready to greet him and to welcome him into our lives.
When we feel weak, help us to be strong.
When we are fearful, help us to be brave.
When we are blind, help us to see the beauty around us.
When we are deaf, help us to hear your message of love.
When we are lame, help us to dance to your music.
When we are silent, help us to listen to you in the stillness.
When we feel lonely, give us friends to hold us.
When we feel bereft, help us to know that you are near.
When we feel angry and hurt, help us to forgive.
When we have hurt others, help us to ask for forgiveness.
When conflict is threatened, make us people of peace.
When darkness surrounds us, make us people of light.
Gracious and loving Father, we offer our prayer to you.
In your mercy, hear us. Amen.

CHRISTMAS CAROL SERVICES DURING ADVENT

Although, in theory, Christmas carols should not be sung until Christmas Eve the reality is, of course, that we sing them from the beginning of Advent. This is particularly so for school children who take part in Christmas carol services before they break up from school for the holidays. This means that churches are often decorated for Christmas quite early in Advent. With careful thought there is no reason why the church cannot be decorated for Advent and also be suitable for the Christmas carol services taking place there.

- An undecorated Christmas tree can be in the church. Maybe children coming in can begin to decorate the tree. This would reinforce the Advent 'getting ready' theme.
- The tree can be decorated entirely with white lights. Christmas is a time to celebrate the coming of Jesus, Light of the World. Advent is the time when we anticipate his coming. Showing children how a small light can always overcome darkness is a very powerful image.
- Many children today will have Advent calendars, often with a completely secular picture on the front, and with chocolates behind the doors. Although these are far removed from the original idea of Advent calendars, they do at least mean that the children are aware of the weeks and days leading up to Christmas. The church can use the idea of Advent calendars as a theme in services leading up to Christmas. Look at the different ways of making and using Advent calendars in this section (pp. 29–32).
- An empty stable scene can be set up in church and the figures gradually added during Advent. This reinforces the idea of waiting and expectation. Who is there still to arrive?

BANNERS USING WORDS FROM ADVENT SUNDAY READINGS

The Gospel readings from Matthew, Mark and Luke for Advent Sunday tell us to *keep watch, because you do not know what day your Lord will come* and *be ready!* The readings from Mark and Luke tell us about the fig tree. *Look at the fig tree, and all the trees. When they sprout leaves, you can see for yourselves and know that summer is near.* We are being told to get ready, to be prepared and to 'do' something.

Looking through magazines we find advertisements which persuade us to 'dine in comfort', 'awaken our senses', 'subscribe', etc. Perhaps we can take a leaf out of the secular world and persuade those who come to our churches during Advent to 'do' something. We can do this by using the words from the readings: 'Be on your guard!' 'Watch!' 'Be alert!' We can add some of our own:

- Are you ready?
- Wake up!
- Be prepared, Jesus is coming!
- Estimated date of arrival 25 Dec.

Use these wake-up calls to make banners, altar frontals and vestments to put around the church. Look at how advertisements use strong contrasting colours so that the words jump out. The traditional colour to use in Advent is purple. The contrasting colour to go with purple is orange, but red or yellow would also stand out well. (See note about using colours in the 'How to ...' chapter.)

BANNERS AND ALTAR FRONTALS FOR ADVENT

Romans 13.11-14

Let us stop doing the things that belong to the dark, and let us take up weapons for fighting in the light.

This reading encourages us to be people of the light. Those who want to do things in secret use the dark to hide their deeds. We are people who should have nothing to hide and should therefore be prepared to let people see what we are doing. Light will always overwhelm darkness. We must always strive to find ways to overwhelm the things of the dark that go on around us. The weapons we are given to use are many: love, joy, hope, cheerfulness, sharing and caring.

   Altar frontals, vestments and banners can all be made in contrasting black on white, or white on black, showing the light overwhelming the dark. Each Sunday in Advent a 'flame' can be attached to a 'candle', like the candles on the Advent ring. In this way you can have a paper or fabric Advent ring instead of a real one.

BANNERS USING THE FIG TREE

Isaiah 61.1–4

They will be like trees that the Lord himself has planted.

The trees that the Lord has planted are full of richness. Banners around the church 'planted like trees' will remind us of the message of good news that the Lord has given us through Jesus coming into the world.

Luke 21.25–36

*Think of the fig tree and all the other trees. When you see their leaves begin-
ning to appear, you know that summer is near. Be on your guard! Be alert!*

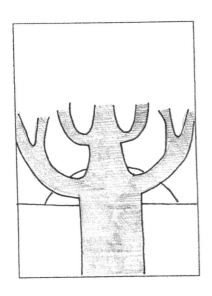

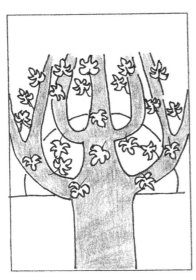
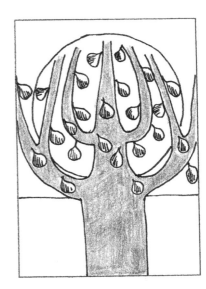

ALTAR FRONTALS OR WALL HANGINGS USING POCKETS

1 Using 5 pockets

These Advent 'calendars' have one pocket for each Sunday in Advent and Christmas Day. Each pocket can contain a gift – something to go on the tree, a candle for the Advent ring or a figure to go in the crib. There can be foot-prints between each pocket to highlight that going through Advent is about going on an **advent**ure. Each pocket can be decorated with a star or with numbers 1 to 5 (or with the dates of each Sunday of Advent and Christmas Day).

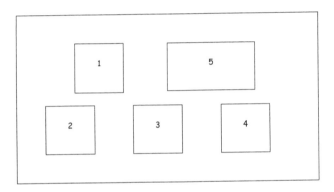

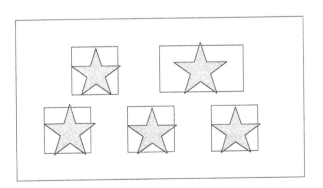

2 Using 5 candle-shaped pockets

This Advent calendar has one candle-shaped pocket for each Sunday in Advent and Christmas Day. Each pocket contains a flame shape. Each week one flame is removed and stuck on its candle – culminating on Christmas Day.

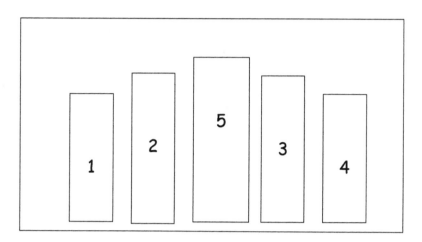

3 Using 25 pockets

Here there are 25 pockets for the days in December leading up to Christmas. Place a small gift in each pocket.

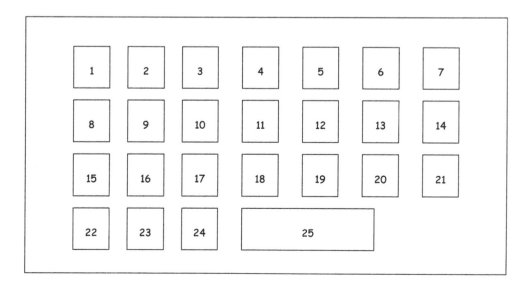

ADVENT RINGS

Advent rings or wreaths have become an accepted part of the decoration in churches for the Advent season. The circle has no beginning or end, reminding us of the never-ending love of God. Candles represent the Light of Christ coming into our dark world. The evergreen, coming from trees that never change whatever the season, remind us of our hope for eternal life with Jesus. Traditionally there are four purple candles, one for each Sunday in Advent. Purple is the liturgical colour we use for repentance and preparation. Some will have a fifth white candle to be lit on Christmas Eve or Day, representing the coming of Jesus into the world.

There are many ways to make Advent rings. A florist will sell bases for rings or wreaths made in wire, straw, twigs or oasis. Before you start to make a ring or wreath reflect on how you will fix the candles to the base. Obviously candles that fall over are dangerous. Other alternatives are round flowerpots or bowls filled with sand or soil. The candles can be pushed into the filling quite safely. A ring made from a paper or polystyrene plate with night-lights stuck on is a very simple way of making a ring, and is a good way to give each person their own ring to take home. These simple rings can be decorated with paper holly leaves and, if you are using each Sunday in Advent for a different theme, the prayers for each theme can be written on the leaves.

Traditionally each Sunday in Advent has a given theme: The People of God, The Prophets, John the Baptist, Mary, Mother of Jesus. But it is always possible to decide your own themes to use during Advent. These might be linked to a run of four sermons on a chosen theme, or you can pick up on situations in the church and local community, or there might be a nation or world situation to focus on for four Sundays. Think creatively. Always make an event of lighting the candles.

- Maybe people who represent different parts of the church community, or children, or invited guests, can each light a candle.
- Use the lighting of the candle as a time for prayer and reflection. Write some specific prayers linked to the theme. Read the same prayers each week as the candles are lit.
- Write a song with simple words linked to the theme and sing it as the candles are lit each week.

Ideas for Themes for Advent Sundays Linked to Lighting Candles on a Ring

- **Follow the traditional themes:**

  The People of God
  The Prophets
  John the Baptist
  Mary

- **Themes linked to the church community:**

  Children
  Young people
  Families
  Older folk

- **Groups in the church:**

  Choir
  Sunday school
  Servers
  Sidespeople

  Cleaners
  Flower arrangers
  Money counters
  Coffee makers

- **Groups in the community:**

  Chemists
  Doctors
  Dentists
  Nurses

  Teachers/Classroom assistants
  Dinner people
  Mentors
  Lollypop men/women

  Refuse collectors
  Street cleaners
  Park gardeners
  Milk/Post deliverers

  Police
  Traffic wardens
  Fire fighters
  Ambulance drivers

Advent rings with stones

This is something a bit different.

1 Have one plate for each Sunday in Advent, each one big enough to have a large candle standing in the middle.
2 Place the plates around the church.
3 Have a large basket full of stones. These can be bought from a garden centre.
4 Place a black indelible pen beside the basket.
5 Invite people to write names of people or situations they want praying for on the stones. These might be linked to the themes chosen for each Sunday in Advent.
6 Place the stones around the base of the candle to be lit that Sunday.
7 Light the candle and say suitable prayers to go with what is written on the stones.
8 Each Sunday in Advent light another candle with another pile of stones.
9 If there is to be a nativity stable in the church for Christmas, at the end of Advent all the stones can be placed in the stable around the crib, so they will be surrounded by the Light of Christ.

'Be prepared' Advent rings

Make an Advent ring using stars. The stars are leading us to the coming of Jesus.

1 Make a circle out of wire.
2 Cut out stars and write words on them, e.g. 'Be prepared'.
3 Sew stars together on a sewing machine leaving some stitches between each one, or stick onto strings.
4 Place evenly onto the wire circle.
5 Hang up.

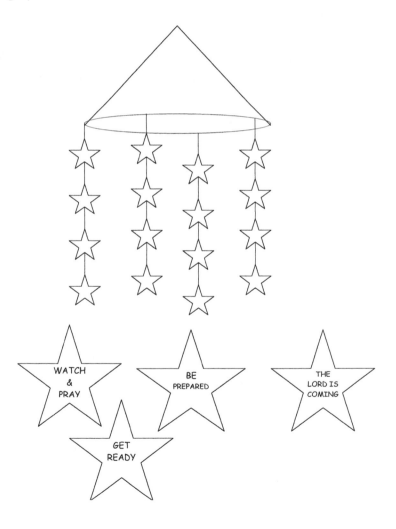

DESIGNS FOR ADVENT STOLES

See the 'How to . . .' chapter for instructions on making a stole. The top designs can be cut out in fabric and then either sewn or stuck on, or a stencil can be made and the design can be sprayed onto the stole. Keep the designs simple and clear. If you do not have purple fabric then spray the background before putting the top design on. Keep the background sprayed fairly lightly so that the top design will stand out well from it.

ADVENT CARDS

Isaiah 2.1–5 Everlasting Peace

He will settle disputes among great nations. They will hammer their swords into ploughs and their spears into pruning-knives. Nations will never again go to war, never prepare for battle again.

This is such a beautiful image. See if you can make some designs for an Advent card. It might be good to work in a circle using the words given in the reading. A circle is never ending so it stands as a symbol of God's never ending love for us. Everyone in the congregation can be given a card on Advent Sunday as a focus for their prayers during the Advent season.

ADVENT CALENDARS

This is an activity for a group. It can be as part of a workshop in the run up to Advent or it can be for a Sunday School or Youth Group meeting. The calendars have five candle doors to open, one for each Sunday of Advent and one for Christmas Day. The calendars can be given out to the congregation on Advent Sunday – so you may need to make lots!

For each calendar you will need one sheet of red A4 card, half a sheet of white A4 paper and some yellow paper. You will need plenty of glue sticks, scissors and thin black pens.

Before the group meets to assemble the calendars you will have to do some preparation. Enlarge the numbered candle template so that the candles fit neatly onto one half of a folded sheet of white A4 paper (ie A5). The bottoms of the candles should line up with one of the short A4 edges. Then photocopy this sheet onto red card. Enlarge the candle template with either scripture verses of pictures in the same way onto white A4 paper. You can do two on a sheet making sure the candle bottoms line up with the short edges of the A4 paper. Cut these in half so that you have A5 sized sheets. (If you like you can blank out the words or pictures from the candle shapes before you photocopy so that people can decorate their own candles.)

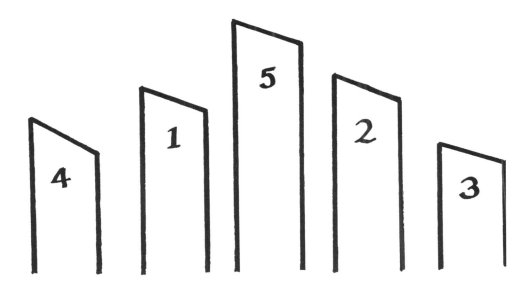

When they saw that the **STAR** had stopped they were overwhelmed with **JOY**
Matthew
2 v 10

The people who walked in darkness have seen **A GREAT LIGHT**
Isaiah
9 v 2

To you is born this day in the City of David **A SAVIOUR** who is **THE MESSIAH THE LORD!**
Luke
2 v 11

A LIGHT to those who sit in darkness and the shadow of death, to guide our feet into the **WAY OF PEACE**
Luke
1 v 79

THE TRUE LIGHT which enlightens everyone was coming into the world.
John
1 v 9

When they saw that the **STAR** had stopped they were overwhelmed with **JOY**
Matthew
2 v 10

The people who walked in darkness have seen **A GREAT LIGHT**
Isaiah
9 v 2

To you is born this day in the City of David **A SAVIOUR** who is **THE MESSIAH THE LORD!**
Luke
2 v 11

A LIGHT to those who sit in darkness and the shadow of death, to guide our feet into the **WAY OF PEACE**
Luke
1 v 79

THE TRUE LIGHT which enlightens everyone was coming into the world.
John
1 v 9

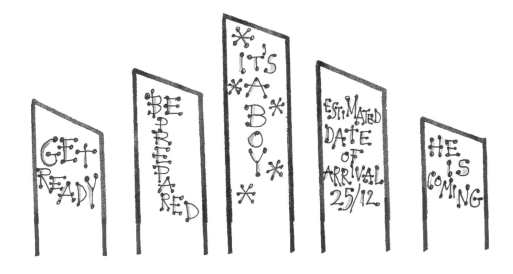

During the workshop give everyone a red A4 sheet of photocopied card, a white A5 sheet of decorated candles (or candles to be decorated), a piece of yellow paper, a pair of scissors, glue and a thin black pen. (If candles are to be decorated you will also need crayons.)

This is what you do:

1   With scissors cut along the right-hand side and top of each candle. Be careful NOT to cut the left-hand side.
2   Fold the red card in half with numbered candles on the outside.
3   Stick the white A5 sheet with decorated candles onto the inside uncut part of the folded red card making sure that the bottoms of the candles line up with the candles you have cut in the red card (if you are decorating your own candles do it now).
4   Carefully place glue all around the candle shapes on the white sheet – being VERY CAREFUL not to put any glue on the candle shapes.
5   Fold the red card down and stick it by pressing very firmly. The candle 'doors' should line up neatly with the candles underneath!
6   Cut flame shapes out of the yellow paper and stick above the candles.
7   Use the thin black pen to draw wicks joining the flames to the candles.

THE JESSE TREE

Isaiah 11.1

A shoot shall come out from the stump of Jesse; from his roots a Branch will bear fruit.

A Jesse Tree is a tree or branches decorated with symbols depicting aspects of the coming of Christ. At the beginning of Advent the tree, or branches, can be erected in church and during the Advent and Christmas seasons symbols can be gradually added.

Get a group together to discuss and think about which symbols you might like to include – look at all the readings for Advent. (The Internet is very helpful – just type 'Jesse Tree' in the search box on your computer and you will find several different web sites.)

The symbols can be drawn and cut out in card and then covered with silver or coloured shiny paper – red and purple for Advent and then silver and white for Christmas. If drawing is difficult copy the pictures on the following pages. Attach cotton loops for hanging on the branches.

Here are some ideas:

Creation	Sun, moon, stars, world map
The Fall	Apples, snake
The Flood	Ark, dove, rainbow
Moses	Burning bush, tablets of the law
King David	Harp, key
King Solomon	Temple
Star of David	Star
Annunciation	Angel
Mary	Lily
Baptism	Water jug
Miracle at Cana	Wine and water jugs
Eucharist	Cup and paten, lamb
Jesus	Fish, star
Chi Rho	XP (the first two letters of the Greek word for Christ)
Peace	Dove
Epiphany	Crowns, stars
Presentation	Candles

The Jesse Tree can stay in the church until the Presentation of Christ in the Temple (Candlemas) on 2 February which marks the end of the Christmas season.

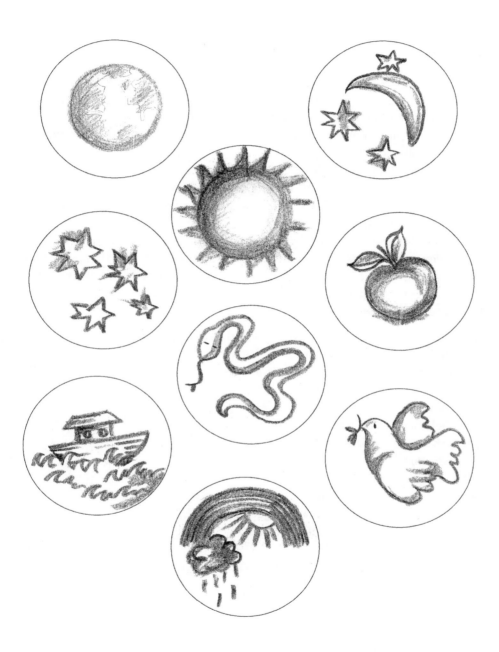

PARISH ACTIVITIES FOR ADVENT

Here are some ideas for 'things to do' in the parish during Advent.

Christmas shoe boxes

Collect and save shoe boxes during the year and fill them with Christmas gifts for an overseas charity. There are several of these around. Look for charities running these schemes on the Internet. The boxes are wrapped in Christmas paper and labelled 'For a boy' or 'For a girl' and the age is given. The charity will tell you exactly how it would like the boxes presented and will come to collect them from you on a specified date.

Imagine a child who has *nothing* and fill the box with treasures – but nothing sharp or liquid. Everyone enjoys doing this – it doesn't matter how old or young you are or whether or not you have children of your own. Many of the children who receive these boxes live on the streets. Filling a shoe box is such fun and so very rewarding. On Christmas morning you can imagine a child somewhere opening *your* box of gifts – it gives a special meaning to Christmas Day.

Christmas gift vouchers

Have a money collection during Advent for specific groups of vulnerable people in the diocese. The money can be turned into gift vouchers which can then be given as Christmas gifts.

Christmas dinner in a box

Another shoe box idea – fill a shoe box with the ingredients of a Christmas dinner and give to the elderly or homeless in your community. The boxes can be wrapped in Christmas paper and a card inside can be signed with love and good wishes from the people of the parish. Be careful to choose tins and packets of food that will not perish, e.g. cans of turkey, potatoes and peas, and Christmas pudding, etc.

Christmas trees

Have a Christmas tree in church. Ask people to bring specific gifts for a local charity – for example, a refuge for the homeless – or for an institution such as a local prison. You might ask people for a tube of toothpaste, a toothbrush, a flannel and soap in a sponge bag. Stars can be hung on the tree as gifts are placed under it.

'Buy a goat'

One major charity runs a scheme to 'recycle goats'. Goats are bought and 'lent' to the poorest families in Africa. Goats produce milk to drink and manure to fertilize the crops – the crop yield increases until there is enough left over to sell – there is then money for clothes, medicine and schools – the goats produce more goats – the family can repay the loan and keep the original goats.

   Draw a large goat on a sheet of paper and pin it up in church. As money to buy a goat is collected colour the goat in until it is complete. Find out all you can about the countries that will receive the goats and find out why donating goats to families in those countries can make such a difference.

Carols and chocolates

Does your parish go carol singing? Here is a novel idea. Instead of collecting money as you go around the houses singing carols, give people chocolates or sweets! Become a church that 'gives' instead of 'receives'. You can, at the same time, give people a Christmas card listing all the Christmas services and events.

Entertaining angels

As Christians we are asked to 'open our homes to strangers'. Christmas is a special time for families – and this can mean it is a hard time for those who do not have them. Are there lonely people in your parish who might welcome an invitation to a Christmas meal? Make a list of those who you think may be alone, and alert those who may be willing to help. Some people do prefer, for whatever reason, to be alone on Christmas Day – so don't press too hard. But others may be delighted and it may make all the difference to what can sometimes be a very lonely time. And it can be fun to have someone different at the Christmas gathering – possibly even angels!

Christmas lunch party

Arrange a Christmas lunch on Christmas Day in your parish room and invite everyone who will be alone at Christmas. Ask people in the congregation to help with providing the food and drink and decorations. Give a small wrapped gift to each person who comes to lunch.

Posadas

Here is a tradition from Mexico. The 'posada' is enacted on each of the nine nights leading up to and including Christmas Eve in nine different houses in the neighbourhood. It enacts the scene from the Bible where Mary and Joseph search for somewhere to stay in Bethlehem. In each house there will be a nativity scene. The family in the house plays the part of 'innkeepers' and the people of the neighbourhood sing a song requesting lodging. Everyone carries a small candle. Children can be dressed as Mary and Joseph and the donkey, or figures of Mary, Joseph and the donkey can be carried.

Traditionally three houses are approached each night, but only the third house invites the group in. Once inside, the group kneels around the nativity scene and says a prayer – traditionally the Rosary – and sings carols. Then there is a party with hot punch for the adults and sweets and games for the children. After Midnight Mass on Christmas Eve the families who have hosted the 'posadas' place the baby Jesus in the manger in their homes. This is followed by a family meal to which friends are invited.

Here is another way to use the 'posada':

1 A few weeks before Advent Sunday put a list up in church for people to sign. There will need to be 24 spaces with room to put addresses and phone numbers.

2 On Advent Sunday, during the service, the first person on the list is given the figures of Mary and Joseph. They are also given two prayer cards, one with a prayer of welcome, and the other with a prayer for departing.

3 The idea is that each day the figures travel from one house to another. The person with the figures is responsible for getting in touch with the next person on the list and making a date and time which suits them both to take the figures round to the next house.

4   On arrival the person receiving the figures is given the prayer of welcome to read.

5   When the person leaves the house he/she reads the prayer of departure.

6   During each Sunday in Advent the people who have looked after the figures that week are asked to stand up and, if possible, speak about what it was like having the figures.

7   On Christmas Day the figures are taken back to church and put in the stable along with the figure of Christ.

This whole exercise, as well as focusing on the coming of Christ, gives an opportunity for people to meet each other, and welcome each other into their homes.

Who is my neighbour?

It is amazing how often we do not know the people who attend our church. Advent gives us a chance to get to know them better. A few weeks before Advent starts, ask as many people in the congregation as possible to join in this exercise.

1   Explain that there will be a large 'Advent calendar' hanging up in church on Advent Sunday. This should be made with 25 pockets. See page 22.

2   Before Advent Sunday everyone who has agreed to join in is given a card.

3   They write their name on the dotted line on the card, and place their card in one of the pockets on the 'Advent calendar', remembering which numbered pocket they put it in.

4   At a given moment in the service everyone goes and takes a card out of a pocket, but not from the numbered pocket that they put their card in.

5   At the end of the service they seek out the person whose name is on the card and tell them that they would like to pray for them that week. It would be good if they could meet up during the week to have a cup of tea or a drink together. This may be someone they have

never met or spoken to before, or it may be someone they know really well. Either way they will agree to pray for that person during the coming week. They can ask the person if there is anything they would particularly like them to pray about.

6   Return the cards to the pockets they came from, so on the next Sunday people can take a different card and the whole thing is done again.

By the end of Advent everyone taking part will have been prayed for by five different people and will have prayed for five different people. They should therefore have met and spoken to ten different people in the church.

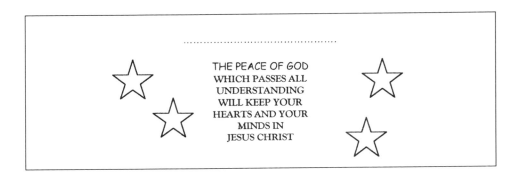

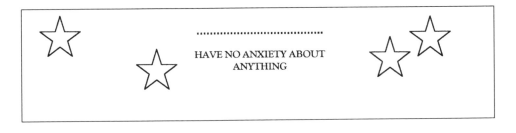

PEW SHEET PUZZLES

Here are two pew sheet puzzles based on Advent Bible readings.

And a little child shall lead them . . .

Eleven animals are mentioned in Isaiah 11.1–10.
  What are they?

1	Sometimes sheep borrow his clothes	(WOLF)
2	Mary had a little one!	(LAMB)
3	This animal sports very smart spots	(LEOPARD)
4	Young goats and children – there's a clue	(KID)
5	Golden ones were once objects of worship	(CALF)
6	Who's the king of the jungle?	(LION)
7	She jumped over the moon	(COW)
8	He can be black or brown and sometimes grizzly	(BEAR)
9	Their tails make very tasty soup!	(OX)
10	Hooded and venomous, they live in holes	(ASP)
11	Not a subtractor!	(ADDER)

The Second Coming – a word search

All the words in this word search are found in the Gospel readings for the first three Sundays of Advent and concern the Second Coming. There are 61 words or phrases. PTO for answer.

B	E	P	R	E	P	A	R	E	D	D	O	O	L	F	K
V	E	L	A	M	E	W	A	L	K	W	J	Q	T	X	I
T	V	W	B	R	E	G	N	E	S	S	E	M	I	K	N
H	W	L	A	Y	C	H	A	F	F	Y	B	V	R	Z	G
R	A	R	E	R	E	L	I	J	A	H	E	J	I	M	D
E	H	N	A	N	E	Q	S	D	R	U	O	H	P	S	O
S	O	N	H	T	E	N	A	M	F	O	N	O	S	T	M
H	N	O	O	M	H	H	I	G	X	R	G	N	Y	S	O
I	J	I	I	B	C	W	A	O	W	E	U	B	L	U	F
N	T	T	R	F	I	O	H	O	J	T	A	C	O	C	G
G	X	A	S	N	S	C	P	D	N	A	R	K	H	O	O
F	J	V	D	J	T	S	U	N	Z	W	D	L	E	L	D
L	Q	L	C	A	L	S	S	E	N	R	E	D	L	I	W
O	M	A	W	I	N	N	O	W	I	N	G	F	O	R	K
O	E	S	D	S	T	A	R	S	M	S	I	T	P	A	B
R	S	E	A	S	Z	T	H	G	I	L	E	U	R	T	T
R	S	X	W	E	T	H	G	I	L	H	T	R	A	E	H
E	I	G	N	N	N	U	F	I	G	T	R	E	E	P	I
P	A	N	G	E	L	G	H	N	E	V	A	E	H	O	E
E	H	K	S	V	S	O	A	Y	R	O	L	G	F	W	F
N	S	N	G	I	S	D	E	S	I	A	R	D	A	E	D
T	L	K	Q	G	B	N	T	W	F	A	T	H	E	R	A
L	E	P	E	R	S	C	L	E	A	N	S	E	D	S	Q
R	A	E	F	O	B	L	I	N	D	S	E	E	C	U	P
X	Q	U	E	F	K	E	E	P	A	L	E	R	T	W	B
W	H	E	A	T	M	N	O	I	T	P	M	E	D	E	R

ANGEL	DEAD RAISED	GLORY	KEEP ALERT	POWERS	THIEF
ARK	DEAF HEAR	GOD	KINGDOM OF	REDEMPTION	THRESHING
BAPTISM	EARTH	GOOD NEWS	GOD	REPENT	FLOOR
BE ON GUARD	ELIJAH	HEAVEN	LAME WALK	SALVATION	TIME
BE PREPARED	FATHER	HILL	LEPERS	SEA	TRUE LIGHT
BEWARE	FEAR	HOLY SPIRIT	CLEANSED	SIGNS	WATCH
BLIND SEE	FIG TREE	HONEY	LIGHT	SON	WATER
CHAFF	FIRE	HOUR	LOCUSTS	SON OF MAN	WHEAT
DAWN	FLOOD	ISAIAH	MESSENGER	STARS	WILDERNESS
DAY	FORGIVENESS	JOHN	MESSIAH	SUN	WIND
			MOON		WINNOWING
			NOAH		FORK
					WRATH

The Second Coming – a word search – Answers

ARE YOU READY FOR CHRISTMAS?

A short play

A group of people standing around talking quietly to each other.

Person 1 asks Person 2:
   'Are you ready for Christmas?'
Person 2, looking very smug, replies:
   'Yes, I have bought *all* my presents.'
Person 1 walks away shaking their head muttering:
   'Yes, but are you really ready?'
Person 2 looks very surprised.

Person 1 asks Person 3:
   'Are *you* ready for Christmas?'
Person 3, looking very smug, replies:
   'Yes, I have bought *all* my presents *and* I have wrapped them all up.'
Person 1 walks away shaking their head muttering:
   'Yes, but are you really ready?'
Person 3 looks very surprised.

Person 1 asks Person 4:
   'Are *you* ready for Christmas?'
Person 4, looking very smug, replies:
   'Yes, I have put up the tree.'
Person 1 walks away shaking their head muttering:
   'Yes, but are you really ready?'
Person 4 looks very surprised.

Person 1 asks Person 5:
   'Are *you* ready for Christmas?'
Person 5, looking very smug, replies:
   'Yes, I have put up the tree *and* put on the lights and decorations.'
Person 1 walks away shaking their head muttering:
   'Yes, but are you really ready?'
Person 5 looks very surprised.

This can be continued with as many people as you have in the group. Think of all the things that we think are important about getting ready for Christmas: buying food and drink and presents, the turkey, writing cards ... the list is endless.

Finally, when **Person 1** has asked each individual if they are ready, everyone stands in a semi-circle in the order that they have answered the questions facing the congregation.

Person 1 asks again, 'Are you *really* ready for Christmas?'
   Going around the semi-circle each person repeats what they have done to get ready using a voice that indicates that they are not amused at being asked again. They have made the effort to get ready, and clearly they are pleased with themselves for being prepared well in advance.

Person 1 then turns to the congregation and asks:
   'Do *you* think they are ready for Christmas?'
The group standing behind **Person 1** all nod their heads – they think they are ready.

Person 1 then asks the congregation:
   'Do you think they are *really* ready for Christmas?'
   'Do you think that they are ready to welcome Christ into their hearts and homes?'
   'Is Christmas about presents and turkeys and trees? Or is it about the Son of God coming among us and showing us a new way?'
   'So are we ready for Christmas?'

All sing **'Are you prepared for Christmas Day?'** to Tallis' Canon

> Are you prepared for Christmas Day
> when Heaven's Child comes here to stay?
> Sing out, clap hands, shout hip hooray!
> The Prince of Peace is on his way.

CHRISTMAS

Christmas has at last arrived and the infant Jesus can be placed in the manger. All the waiting is over, Jesus is born, and at last we can sing verse 7 of 'O come, all ye faithful!' Many of us may have worshipped at a midnight service and may have been very late to bed on Christmas Eve – and then woken up very early on Christmas Day. It is a time for celebration and families. It can also be a time of stress and exhaustion for those who have worked so hard to get everything ready in time. Not everyone is held in the loving embrace of a family – and this is a time to remember those who are alone, maybe for the first time at Christmas, or those who are away from home and need gathering up.

This part includes examples of mosaic and patchwork banners, candles to decorate and give away, instructions for assembling crib scenes, birthday cards for Jesus, and even an instant play to perform on Christmas morning in church. All you need are some props and willing participants on the day.

READINGS FOR CHRISTMAS DAY

Years A, B and C

Any of the following sets of readings may be used on the evening of Christmas Eve and on Christmas Day. Set 3 should be used at some service during the celebration.

Set 1

Isaiah 9.2–7
Psalm 96
Titus 2.11–14
Luke 2.1–14 (15–20)

Set 2

Isaiah 62.6–12
Psalm 97
Titus 3.4–7
Luke 2.(1–7) 8–20

Set 3

Isaiah 52.7–10
Psalm 98
Hebrews 1.1–4 (5–12)
John 1.1–14

HYMNS AND SONGS FOR CHRISTMAS

Details of these hymnbooks and song books are on pages xxi–xxiv.

Beneath a Travelling Star

Holy child, how still you lie
How faint the stable lantern's light
The hush of midnight here below

Carol Praise

In a byre near Bethlehem
Let it be to me
Light of the world (Here I am to worship)
Like a flicker in the darkness
Lord, you left your throne
O come all you children
O holy night
Still, still, still
When shepherds watched and angels sang

Heaven Shall Not Wait

Sing a different song
The aye carol

Hymns of Glory, Songs of Praise

Before the world began one Word was there
Jesus is born
Love came down at Christmas
One day an angel here on this earth

Hymns Old and New: New Anglican Edition

At this time of giving
Be still, for the presence of the Lord
Born in the night, Mary's child

Cloth for the cradle
Come on and celebrate
For Mary, mother of our Lord
See him lying on a bed of straw (Calypso Carol)

Laudate

Carol at the manger
Gaudete
Infant holy
Jesus, Saviour, holy child
'Twas in the moon of wintertime
What shall we give

Liturgical Hymns Old and New

Angels we have heard in heaven
Christ, be our light

Sing Glory

Come and sing the Christmas story
Jesus Christ the Lord is born
Like a candle flame
This child
What if the one who shapes the stars

Songs and Prayers from Taizé

Gloria, gloria
Jubilate Deo

Veni Emmanuel

He came down that we may have love (with Gloria)
Unto us a child is given

CHILDREN'S NATIVITY SONG

Tune: Mulberry Bush

A song for children in a nativity – all the verses can be sung by all the children or the children taking part in the story can sing their own special verses.

1   A star is shining in Bethlehem,
    Bethlehem, Bethlehem,
    a star is shining in Bethlehem
    on a tiny child in a manger.

2   Mary and Joseph are loving him,
    loving him, loving him,
    Mary and Joseph are loving him,
    the tiny child in the manger.

3   The sheep and cattle will keep him warm,
    keep him warm, keep him warm,
    the sheep and cattle will keep him warm,
    the tiny child in the manger.

4   The angels sing of peace on earth,
    peace on earth, peace on earth,
    the angels sing of peace on earth
    because of the child in the manger.

5   The shepherds leap and dance with joy,
    dance with joy, dance with joy,
    the shepherds leap and dance with joy
    for the tiny child in the manger.

6   What are the gifts the wise men bring,
    wise men bring, wise men bring,
    what are the gifts the wise men bring
    to the tiny child in the manger?

7   Gold and myrrh and frankincense,
    frankincense, frankincense,
    gold and myrrh and frankincense
    for the tiny child in the manger.

8   Join with us as we welcome him,
    welcome him, welcome him,
    join with us as we welcome him,
    the tiny child in the manger.

9   Alleluia, praise to him,
    praise to him, praise to him,
    alleluia, praise to him,
    the tiny child in the manger.

© Jan Brind

CHRISTMAS HYMN

Tune: All for Jesus or Laus Deo (Redhead No. 46) 87 87

1 Heaven rings with joyful tidings,
   Angels sing of peace on earth;
   Love and joy and hope and promise,
   Mary's boy child brought to birth!

2 In the speaking of your story,
   In the singing of your song;
   In the silence of our praying
   Grant the peace for which we long.

3 In our tears and in our sorrow,
   In our sharing and our care;
   In our laughter and our gladness
   We believe that you are near.

4 In a world where many hunger
   You shall offer living bread;
   When the thirsty long for water
   You shall be the fountainhead.

5 At this Christmastide we welcome
   God with us, Emmanuel;
   Prince of Peace for our salvation,
   Holy Child with us to dwell.

6 Heaven rings with joyful tidings,
   Angels sing of peace on earth;
   Love and joy and hope and promise,
   Mary's boy child brought to birth!

© Jan Brind

PRAYERS FOR CHRISTMAS DAY

On this joyful Christmas Day we welcome Jesus the Christ into our lives and listen to the message of good news that he brings. We pray for the whole church of God, for our priests and teachers and all who inspire and lead us in the ways of love and truth.
May your light shine,
And reveal to us your glory.

We pray for the whole of God's beautiful world. May we become better stewards of creation. We pray that it may not be too late to heal those places we have damaged by our greed and negligence. Give us eyes to see beyond our own horizons.
May your light shine,
And reveal to us your glory.

We pray for the hungry of the world. May we find ways to share the earth's bounty more equally. May we find practical means to support and encourage the campaign for trade justice. Give us hearts and minds to respond to the cry and needs of the poor.
May your light shine,
And reveal to us your glory.

We pray for our families and loved ones. May we be bearers of peace in our own homes and with our neighbours. Give us voices to sing in harmony and blessing with those around us.
May your light shine,
And reveal to us your glory.

We pray for those who suffer in mind, body or spirit. May we be symbols of light to those whose lives are in darkness. You have given us eyes and ears to notice the pain around us. You have given us hands to do your healing work. Help us to use them.
May your light shine,
And reveal to us your glory.

We give thanks for all the saints and those who have gone before us. Make our feet to follow in their paths so that we may continue their good works. Be with us this day and in the days to come that we may know your presence with us.

May your light shine,

And reveal to us your glory.

LONG HANGING CHRISTMAS BANNERS

Isaiah 9.6

For to us a child is born, to us a son is given, and the government will be on his shoulders. And he will be called 'Wonderful Counsellor, Mighty God, Everlasting Father, Prince of Peace.'

These amazing words are wonderful to hang on the walls as banners. Make one long thin banner for each word or phrase and hang them either together or down the pillars in the church.

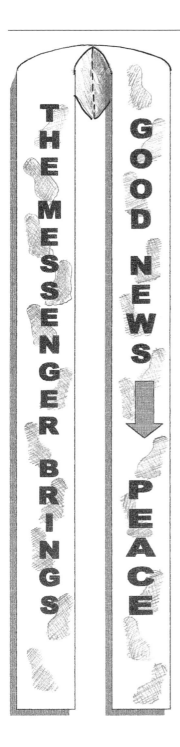

BANNERS, FRONTALS AND STOLES USING THE GOOD NEWS

Isaiah 52.7

How beautiful on the mountains are the feet of those who bring good news, who proclaim peace.

This reading from Isaiah gives a wonderful image of the messenger rushing in having run across the mountains. He is out of breath, but he has 'good news' to tell. The message is the news of peace. He announces victory and says, 'Your God reigns'. The response to this announcement is 'shouting together with joy'.

Make a banner, altar frontal or stole with the 'good news' message. Before putting the message on the fabric or paper have fun painting the bottoms of people's feet and then ask them to walk all over the background. Then stick or spray the letters on.

MOSAIC BANNER

Make a mosaic out of paper. Cut out paper squares all the same size. Use light-coloured paper descending through shades of the same colour, getting darker and darker. Working from the middle use the lightest coloured squares and then work out towards the edge getting darker as the squares get nearer the edge. When the background has stuck and dried, cut out the words 'Jesus Light of the World' and stick them onto the mosaic.

PATCHWORK BANNER

John 1.4–5: The Light of the World

The Word was the source of life, and this life brought light to mankind. The light shines in the darkness, and the darkness has never put it out.

Christmas is so often seen as the time of a babe in a stable. But it should also be seen as the time when Jesus came into the world as the 'Light of the World'. Take this as a theme for Christmas time.

   A patchwork 'quilt' banner is an excellent way to get a group of people to make a banner together. For instructions on how to make a patchwork banner see the 'How to ...' chapter in the back of the book.

1   Decide where the banner will hang and how big it will be.
2   Decide on a colour scheme both for the background and the patches.
3   Prepare the background for hanging.
4   Decide on the design of the banner. What shape will the patches be and how will they be placed on the background?
5   Decide how big the patches will be. Cut them out in fairly heavy paper.
6   Give each person a 'patch'. Ask them to put a design on it that represents something to do with light. This could be with symbols or words. The design could be drawn, cut out and stuck on, or painted. Whatever method used it needs to be big and bold.
7   Collect all the patches and decide in what order they will be placed on the background.
8   Stick the paper patches onto the background and hang up the banner.

BANNERS USING 'THE LIGHT OF THE WORLD' THEME

Think of different ways of using the theme of Jesus, Light of the World on banners. The words can go all around the world, or the light can be shining out.

Here are some ideas:

CANDLES

If you are using the theme of 'Jesus, Light of the World', candles are an obvious symbol to illustrate this. Put these words onto candles. See how to decorate candles with words in the 'How to ...' chapter. The candles can either be large ones to put in the church, or smaller ones that everyone can take home. If using small night lights write 'Jesus, Light of the World' onto small strips of sticky paper. Wrap these papers onto the metal part of each candle.

JESUS LIGHT OF THE WORLD

MAKING CRIB SCENES

Luke 2

This is the only detailed description of the birth of Christ that is given to us. It is a story that we all know so well: the birth in the stable and the shepherds coming to see the baby. Many churches have a stable with the figures from the story placed somewhere prominent in the building. The figures can be beautifully carved from wood or made from plaster. They are often something that the church has used for years and sadly, often, they have got rather tired looking and out of date. It is worth checking the figures well before Christmas to see if any repairs need doing. Repainting or even just cleaning the figures can make them look more beautiful. Rethink how they will be displayed. Can they be put in another place in the church so people will see them anew? Do not get stuck in the 'But we have always done it like that' mode. We often stop seeing things when we have always done them in the same way.

Making 3D figures for a crib

It is not difficult to make crib figures. The simplest way to make a figure is by using a plastic bottle 'body', with a polystyrene 'head' stuck on the neck of the bottle. Polystyrene balls can easily be bought from craft shops. Make sure that there is something heavy in the bottom of the bottle before the head is stuck on, like sand or soil. This will stop the bottle falling over. Wrap fabric round the bottle and over the head. Draw on a face. A man can be given a beard made from cotton wool. Smaller plastic bottles can be made into children, and if laid on their sides they can be cattle or sheep!

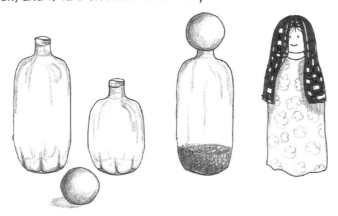

Making a paper crib to hang on the wall or as an altar frontal

If there is not enough room in church for a stable with figures in it, then make a paper nativity scene. This can either go on the wall or be used as an altar frontal. On a large sheet of paper draw the stable. Cut out and decorate the figures to go in the stable. Keep the shapes very simple. Add arms to each basic shape, and decorate the clothing on each figure with paints or felt pens.

Alternatively, let each person make his or her own stable and put their own figures in it. As the Christmas season continues they can gradually add different figures, starting with the Holy Family, and then each Sunday adding the rest of the figures – shepherds and sheep and, at Epiphany, the wise men.

LARGE DOWELLING OR BAMBOO STAR

For a star to have a real impact it needs to be big. Often stars made from card became floppy and just do not have the impact that is needed. Make a star from pieces of dowelling or bamboo sticks. Because the framework is rigid it can be made really big and will look good from all sides.

1   Cut five pieces of wood 50cm (20in) long (or a length of your choice).
2   Fix each length at the points as shown in the diagram. A fixed to B, B to C, C to D, D to E, E to A. Secure them either with wire or a small nail.
3   Spray or paint the wood with gold or silver.
4   Wrap tinsel round the whole structure.
5   Hang up over the stable, on fishing line wire, so the thread does not show.

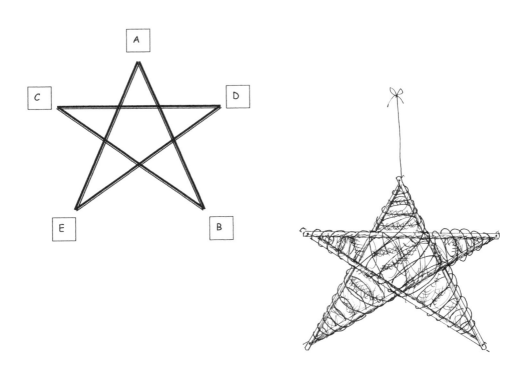

USING PUPPETS TO TELL THE CHRISTMAS STORY

The Christmas story is so well-known that one of the most effective ways to bring it alive is to tell it using puppets.

There are many different ways to make the puppets, from very simple ones like spoon puppets, which just need some sticking, to more complicated ones like glove puppets, which need sewing. Decide which type of puppets will be made and then which of the characters from the Christmas story will be used. A screen of some kind will be needed for the puppeteers to stand behind. If only a few people are involved, using a pulpit can be very effective. It is often raised up above the congregation so the puppets can easily be seen. If more people are involved, then a large sheet hung up across the church can also work. As it is sometimes difficult to hear voices in church it may be better to have a narrator to read the story clearly with the puppeteers enacting the story as it unfolds. For instructions for making puppets see the 'How to . . .' chapter at the back of the book.

ADVENT, CHRISTMAS AND EPIPHANY SEASON RINGS

In the Advent part of this book there is a section on making and using Advent rings. These rings are often removed from the church after Christmas Day. However, they can be used as a focus point right up to, and including, The Presentation of Christ in the Temple (Candlemas). For each festival new items can be added to the ring to highlight that festival.

The progress from Advent Sunday to Candlemas could be:

- *Advent Sunday* Four candles set in a circle of greenery or a circle of stones.
- *Christmas Day* A large candle is set in the centre representing the Light of Christ coming into our midst.
- *The Epiphany* Add gold, frankincense and myrrh to the circle. Use gold Christmas tree baubles and an incense burner, frankincense and myrrh bought from a shop selling essential oils, to represent the gifts brought by the wise men.
- *The Baptism of Christ* Add a jug of water and a dove to the circle. This could be a simple dove cut out of card and placed on a stick or a small, bought, figure of a bird covered in white feathers, or someone might have a white china dove. These represent the water of the River Jordan and the Holy Spirit which 'descended like a dove'.
- *Candlemas* Add more candles around the circle. This could be circle of night lights around the outside of the original circle representing Simeon's words 'a light to reveal your will to the Gentiles, and bring glory to your people Israel'.

At the end of the Candlemas service the candles are blown out and the circle is packed away, along with the rest of the Advent, Christmas and Epiphany seasonal items.

PARISH ACTIVITIES FOR CHRISTMAS DAY

Birthday cards

Make a birthday card for Jesus. It is, after all, his birthday and this is what we have been looking forward to in Advent and what we are now celebrating on Christmas Day. When we have birthdays they are special and exciting. We bless people on their birthdays and make them feel loved. The church will probably be filled with flowers and candles – add balloons and streamers!

The design for the birthday card can be photocopied onto coloured card. Before folding the card over cut along the top of the big balloon with a craft knife. Now fold the card. The balloon will stand up from the card. Make enough cards for everyone in the congregation and, if possible, enough for everyone in the parish. Give them out on Christmas Day – or ask people to pop them through their neighbours' letterboxes! It is not generally realized that this season of celebration extends through Epiphany until the 2 February when we celebrate The Presentation of Christ in the Temple, or 'Candlemas'. It might be good to explain this inside the card. The idea that decorations

have to be put away on 6 January, Twelfth Night, is a relatively new idea. Candlemas marks the time when we turn away from all that has happened in the birth narrative and begin to look towards Holy Week and the cross. Put the times of the services from Christmas Day until Candlemas in the back of the card to encourage people to take part fully in both the Christmas and Epiphany seasons.

Christmas star cake

Make a special cake to have on Christmas Day after the service. Use a star-shaped tin and your favourite recipe. Decorate it with frosting and coloured chocolate sprinkles and put one candle on it for Jesus, Light of the World. Sing 'Happy Birthday' to Jesus and ask a child to blow out the candle.

Hospitality

Remember that on Christmas Day many people will be on their own. This may be through choice, but very often it is a time of great loneliness. Even a last-minute invitation to a Christmas Day meal is sometimes graciously accepted. Be aware of the lonely people around you.

Light of the World cupcakes

Make a batch of cupcakes for everyone to share on Christmas Day – see the following recipe. Sing verse 5 of 'One more step along the world I go'. Everyone can have a candle to blow out!

LIGHT OF THE WORLD CUPCAKES

You will need 20 paper cases, 20 birthday candleholders and 20 candles

Oven temperature: 375°F, 190°C, gas mark 5

Ingredients:

100g (4oz) soft margarine
100g (4oz) caster sugar
200g (8oz) self-raising flour
1 level teaspoon baking powder
1 teaspoon vanilla essence
1 egg

200g (8oz) icing sugar
50g (2oz) cocoa powder
125g (5oz) soft butter

Method:

Cream together the margarine, sugar, vanilla essence and egg. Add the sifted flour and baking powder. Beat mixture for 2 to 3 minutes. Spoon the mixture into paper cases and place them on a baking tray. Put in the oven for 15 minutes or until golden brown and firm to the touch. Remove from the oven and place on a rack to cool.

Sieve the icing sugar and cocoa powder into a bowl and add the soft butter. Mix together until soft and creamy. Spread chocolate icing onto the cooled cakes. Place one birthday candleholder and candle in each cupcake.

This makes about 20 cakes.

A CHILD IS BORN

A simple interactive story about the birth of Jesus.

Here is a short drama suitable for acting from scratch during a Christmas service in church. All you need are the children to take part and some pre-gathered 'props'. Decide where in the church you want to stage the nativity scene. As the story unfolds invite children from the congregation to come forward and take part. As they come forward talk about the characters in the story and how they would feel. Help them to choose the right props. Show them where to stand, sit or kneel.

In a land far away, in a town called Nazareth in Galilee, a young woman named Mary, and her husband Joseph, set out on a journey that will lead them to Bethlehem where their names will be registered in a census. Mary is soon to have a baby. She rides on a donkey and Joseph leads her.

From the congregation: Mary, Joseph and a donkey
Props: A blue shawl, a teatowel and tie, donkey ears
The journey is long and it is wintertime. Mary and Joseph are pleased to reach Bethlehem safely. The town is noisy and crowded with people. Joseph is unable to find room in any of the inns, but eventually he is shown to a stable where animals shelter.

From the congregation: Various animals
Props: A large star, two stools, a box filled with hay, a doll wrapped in cloth, sets of animals ears
During the night Mary's baby boy is born and she wraps him in cloth and lays him on the hay in the animals' manger. The animals quietly watch what is taking place. They keep the little family warm with their breath. The baby is named Jesus. Suddenly the sky is filled with starlight.
   There are shepherds on the hills around Bethlehem looking after their sheep.

From the congregation: Two or three shepherds, sheep, angels
Props: Teatowels, ties and shepherds' crooks, sheep ears, a toy lamb and a flute for the shepherds, circles of tinsel for the angels' heads
Suddenly the sky is filled with the sound of beautiful singing. Angels appear to the shepherds singing 'Glory to God in the highest, and peace to his people

on earth! Do not be afraid! We bring good news. Today in Bethlehem a special child is born. His name is Jesus and he is the Prince of Peace. You will find him lying in a manger. Go and see him!' Some of the shepherds leave their sheep on the hillside and hurry to find Jesus. When they find him they kneel down and offer gifts to him – a lamb and a flute. They are filled with joy.

There are others travelling to Bethlehem at this time. Wise men, or magi, from the East have been following a star – they believe that it will lead them to the Messiah, promised by the prophets from long ago.

From the congregation: At least three wise men
Props: Suitable headdresses, gifts representing gold, myrrh and frankincense
The wise men arrive at the stable and offer their precious gifts of gold, myrrh and frankincense to Jesus. They kneel at the manger.

Soon word spreads in Bethlehem that something very special has happened. Children gather at the stable to welcome Jesus.

From the congregation: All the children who have not already come forward and who would like to take part
Props: Musical instruments – tambourines and bells
Ever since that special night over two thousand years ago people all over the world have celebrated the birth of Jesus, the baby who came into the world in poverty to bring us love and joy and hope. We call this celebration Christmas.

Now let us all sing a gentle song to welcome Jesus.

Everyone sings: 'A star is shining in Bethlehem'

EPIPHANY

The season of Epiphany has three separate feast days. First the Epiphany itself when the wise men, having followed a bright star, arrive at the manger to worship Jesus and present their gifts of gold, myrrh and frankincense. We then jump ahead in the Gospel story to the Baptism of Christ and the account of Jesus being baptized by John in the Jordan River. The Presentation of Christ in the Temple – also called Candlemas – is the third feast we look at in this section. The word 'epiphany' is derived from the Greek word *phaino* meaning 'show'. Jesus is 'shown' or 'revealed' to the wise men, to John the Baptist, and to Simeon and Anna in the temple at Jerusalem. All these had been waiting patiently for Jesus to appear.

In this part we have some fun with stars, we consider ways of engaging with refugees and asylum seekers, and we finally put away the symbols that have decorated our churches since the beginning of Advent.

The Epiphany

READINGS FOR THE EPIPHANY

Years A, B and C

Isaiah 60.1–6
Psalm 72.(1–9) 10–15
Ephesians 3.1–12
Matthew 2.1–12

HYMNS AND SONGS FOR THE EPIPHANY

Details of these hymnbooks and song books are on pages xxi–xxiv.

Beneath a Travelling Star

Come, watch with us
How silent waits the listening earth

Liturgical Hymns Old and New

What child is this

Sing Glory

Wise men of old came seeking
Wise men, they came to look for wisdom

Veni Emmanuel

What shall I bring

PRAYERS FOR THE EPIPHANY

For star followers that they may discover their dream,
Lord of all,
Hear our prayer.

For travellers and searchers that they may find peace,
Lord of all,
Hear our prayer.

For the homeless that they may find shelter this day,
Lord of all,
Hear our prayer.

For refugees and asylum seekers that they may find a
place of acceptance and safety,
Lord of all,
Hear our prayer.

For those in danger that they may find someone to trust,
Lord of all,
Hear our prayer.

For those who find themselves weary of life that they
may find the courage and energy to change direction,
Lord of all,
Hear our prayer.

For those who are in the darkness of despair that they may
recognize and rejoice in 'Epiphany moments',
Lord of all,
Hear our prayer.

For bearers of precious gifts that their gifts may be
accepted graciously and used in your name,
Lord of all,
Hear our prayer.

For ourselves in this New Year that we may resolve to follow
more closely your way of love and joy and peace in our lives,
Lord of all,
Hear our prayer.

BANNERS AND ALTAR FRONTALS
FOR THE EPIPHANY

Isaiah 60.1–6

Arise, shine, for your light has come, and the glory of the Lord rises upon you. Nations will come to your light, and kings to the brightness of your dawn.

This conjures up a wonderful image of people coming from all over the world being drawn to the One Light. Make a banner or altar frontal to illustrate these words. This could be made in paper or fabric.

1   Decide on the shape of the banner or altar frontal.
2   Cut out a huge yellow sun – this could go over the edge of the main background shape.
3   Draw, and then cut out, people dancing, either in black fabric or paper, so they are silhouetted against the yellow sun. These figures need to get smaller, so it looks as if they are going towards the light. To do this draw the outline of several fairly large figures on a piece of white paper, then reduce them to size on a photocopier.
4   Place the outline picture over the black fabric or paper and cut round the outline.
5   Stick the figures on the background in descending order going towards the Light.
6   Cut out the letters for the words and stick on.

STAR FOLLOWERS

The magi, or wise men, thought to be astrologers, took a risk when they set out on their journey. They had no map, only a star. They did not know where they would end up or what dangers they would encounter on the way. But they trusted that they would find the promised king at the end of their journey. They believed that they were being led by the star to see this king.

The example given to us by the wise men, that we should trust and have faith, and that all shall be well, is important to hold onto as we journey through our lives. If we put our trust in Jesus we will be guided on the way; because he is 'The Way'.

So we must be like the wise men, star followers, believing that we are guided and guarded as we journey through life, and that we will be led to the right places.

Make badges for everyone in church to wear.

1   Cut out star shapes in card and print the following words on them:
    'I am a star follower' or 'I am a follower of The Way'.
2   Stick a safety pin on the back of each one.
3   Give a star badge to everyone in church to encourage them to 'follow the star' that led the wise men to Jesus. We will find Jesus wherever we go.

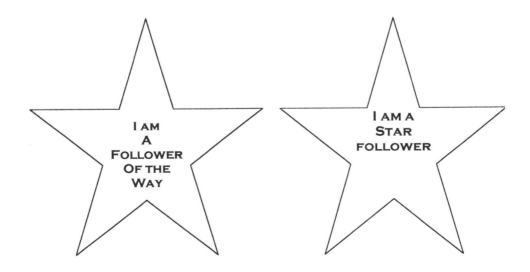

PARISH ACTIVITIES FOR THE EPIPHANY

Entertaining refugees and asylum seekers

We are told that the magi, possibly astrologers, journeyed a great distance following a star that they believed would lead them to the promised 'King of the Jews'. They brought with them gold, a gift for a king, incense for deity, and myrrh, a spice given to someone going to die. These are symbolic gifts – hardly gifts for a baby – but gifts that foretold the events of Jesus' life and death. Epiphany is a time of recognition – and revelation. We talk of 'epiphany moments' when something suddenly becomes clear. King Herod asked the magi to tell him where Jesus was so that he, too, could worship him. But the magi, being warned in a dream that Herod meant to harm Jesus, returned home by another route. Joseph, too, was warned in a dream that Herod wanted to kill Jesus so he journeyed with Mary and Jesus to Egypt. They became refugees.

Many people in today's society find themselves journeying to another country to escape danger. Very often they do not want to leave their homes and familiar patterns of life but they have no choice. They may find themselves, through necessity, in a strange land, trying to speak a strange language, and dealing with unfamiliar social customs. Yet, very often, the gifts these people bring us are much needed. How can we welcome and embrace these strangers in our midst? One way is with hospitality. Are there any refugees or asylum seekers in your community or in nearby communities? Organize and invite them to a meal. Ask each member of the congregation to bring two plates of food – one for themselves and one for a guest. Make it simple by specifying what the lunch should be so that everyone has much the same. Provide coffee and tea. Or ask the congregation to 'bring and share' plates of food. Invite someone who is involved with the care of refugees and asylum seekers in your area to come and speak in a church service.

New Year resolutions

New Year resolutions are also about 'changing direction'. Ask everyone in the congregation to write their new resolutions on pieces of paper. Place the folded pieces of paper in a basket and present them as part of the offertory on the first Sunday in the New Year.

Offering of gifts

What gifts would we bring to Jesus? Ask each person in the congregation to write a special gift that they would like to give Jesus on a piece of paper. Place the folded pieces of paper in a basket and place them next to the crib in the church. *Don't forget to place the magi and their gifts in the stable now.*

Epiphany cake

In Belgium on Epiphany Sunday all the cake shops sell sponge Epiphany cakes. These are plain sponge cakes with one nut inside. Around the outside of each cake is a golden paper crown. At Epiphany the family gathers together and eats the cake. The person who has the nut in their slice is the king or queen for the day and is allowed to wear the paper crown!

This idea can easily be introduced into church. Before the Sunday service make a large round plain sponge cake with one nut in it. Cut out a paper crown and place it around the outside of the cake. At the end of the service tell everyone that there is one nut in the cake. When everyone is having coffee, offer round slices of the Epiphany cake. The person who has the nut in their slice is given the paper crown to wear and a golden box full of chocolates or homemade biscuits to take home. If it is difficult to find a gold-coloured box, then it is very easy to cover a small box with gold-coloured paper.

CARDS FOR THE EPIPHANY

Make Epiphany cards to give to everyone in church to encourage them to recognize that life is a journey of change, and by accepting the changes we allow God to reach out to us and help us to take risks. It is through those changes that we often learn more and our lives are enriched. It is when we want to stay were we are that we stagnate and stop growing. Cardinal Newman's words illustrate this so well.

Make a card for everyone in Church, or print the words on the front of the pew sheet.

To live
Is to
Change
To be
Perfect
Is to
Change often

Cardinal Newman

The Baptism of Christ

READINGS FOR THE BAPTISM OF CHRIST

Year A

Isaiah 42.1–9
Psalm 29
Acts 10.34–43
Matthew 3.13–17

Year B

Genesis 1.1–5
Psalm 29
Acts 19.1–7
Mark 1.4–11

Year C

Isaiah 43.1–7
Psalm 29
Acts 8.14–17
Luke 3.15–17, 21–22

HYMNS AND SONGS FOR THE BAPTISM OF CHRIST

Details of these hymnbooks and song books are on pages xxi–xxiv.

Hymns Old and New: New Anglican Edition

Spirit of the living God

Laudate

Songs of thankfulness and praise

Songs and Prayers from Taizé

Veni Sancte Spiritus

Songs of Fellowship

O let the Son of God enfold you
Such love

BAPTISM SONG

Tune: Epiphany 11 10 11 10

1   Gathered together to witness a birthing,
    Water and Spirit to make all things new;
    Clothing, refreshing, reviving, anointing,
    Holy reminders of faith strong and true.

2   All who are lost in the shadows of darkness
    Now shall be bathed in your soft, shining light;
    God our Creator, you bring us to wholeness,
    Fit for your Church as the body of Christ.

3   Open our eyes so we see you more clearly,
    Sharpen our ears so your call may be heard;
    Widen our hearts so we love you more dearly,
    Make us a people who live by your word.

4   Jesus, our Lord, in his pain and his dying
    Carried our sin so that we may be freed;
    Rising again to give peace everlasting,
    Leaving the Spirit, as he had decreed.

5   Pilgrims rejoicing in baptismal blessing,
    Formed by the Father, redeemed by the Son;
    Sent out to witness the gospel unending,
    Led by the Spirit in whom we are one.

6   Given a new name, and strength for the journey,
    Claiming in baptism promise foretold;
    This is our calling, and this is our story,
    God's living stones being Christ in the world.

© Jan Brind

PRAYERS FOR THE BAPTISM OF CHRIST

Let us pray to God the Father who calls us and knows each one of us by name.

We pray for our archbishops, bishops and priests, and for all who witness to the Christian faith. We give thanks for those who have inspired and taught us by word and example, in story and picture and song. We give thanks for prophets and preachers, for authors and poets, for artists and musicians. We give thanks for parents and godparents and all those who have walked with us and kindled the flame of faith in our lives.
Father in heaven,
Fill us with your spirit.

We give thanks for our brothers and sisters in church communities through-out the world. By baptism we are members of one family. May we learn more about each other so that we can truly become a visible and united sign of Christ's presence here on earth.
Father in heaven,
Fill us with your spirit.

We pray for peace in your troubled world. May your Holy Spirit guide leaders of all nations in the ways of truth and justice and wisdom. Where there is conflict bring harmony, where there is darkness bring light and where there is misunderstanding bring forgiveness and compassion.
Father in heaven,
Fill us with your spirit.

Bless our families and friends, and all our neighbours. We give thanks for children and godchildren and for the joy that they bring. We pray for the work of the aid agencies in the worldwide church who bring hope to the many thousands of children in the world who live on the streets and to those who are born unwanted and unloved.
Father in heaven,
Fill us with your spirit.

Bring comfort to those who suffer in body, mind or spirit. We remember those who have died in the faith of Christ. Give strength and hope to those who grieve. May we have the courage to reach out in love to each other, and recognize that being a member of your Church means living your way, your truth and your life.

Father in heaven,

Fill us with your spirit.

Candlemas – The Presentation of Christ in the Temple

READINGS FOR CANDLEMAS

Years A, B and C

Malachi 3.1–5
Psalm 24.(1–6) 7–10
Hebrews 2.14–18
Luke 2.22–40

HYMNS AND SONGS FOR CANDLEMAS

Details of these hymnbooks and song books are on pages xxi–xxiv.

Be Still and Know

Day is done, but love unfailing
The Lord is my light

Hymns Old and New: New Anglican Edition

Faithful vigil ended
I, the Lord of sea and sky

Laudate

Christ, be our light
Now let your servant go in peace
The light of Christ

Sing Glory

Like a candle flame

Songs and Prayers from Taizé

The Lord is my light

Songs from Taizé

Lord Jesus Christ, your light shines within us
Nunc dimittis (Let your servant now go in peace)
Your word, O Lord, is a light

Veni Emmanuel

Now let your servants, Lord, depart in peace

PRAYERS FOR CANDLEMAS

Give everyone a candle and drip shield to hold at the beginning of the service. Just before the prayers begin the candles are lit.

As we gather together during this turning point in the Gospel story of Jesus, let us offer our prayers to God, the Father.

Heavenly Father, through your prophet Malachi you promised to send a messenger with a new covenant who would prepare your way before you and would be revealed by Simeon and Anna as a light to the Gentiles and the glory of your people Israel. We give thanks for the faithful vigil of Simeon and Anna in the temple. We give thanks for the wisdom and faithfulness of all older people. May we learn from their example of patience and perseverance.

For the Light of Christ,
We pray to the Lord.

We pray that the Light of Christ may shine throughout your world. May it illumine the dark places where fear and pain abide. May it shine on people of every race and colour and creed.

For the Light of Christ,
We pray to the Lord.

We pray for ourselves, our loved ones, our families and our neighbours. May your light be ever about us as we strive to do your will.

For the Light of Christ,
We pray to the Lord.

We pray for the sick and needy, for the lonely and bereft, and for those who live in the shadow of death. May we be bearers of your light to all who suffer. We pray for those who have died that they may be gathered into the eternal light of heaven.

For the Light of Christ,
We pray to the Lord.

As we now turn away from the Christmas and Epiphany seasons and begin to journey towards Holy Week send us out as children of light, to live and work to your praise and glory.

Amen

Candles are extinguished at the end of the prayers.

PARISH ACTIVITIES FOR CANDLEMAS

Who is he, this King of Glory?

Psalm 24.7–10 gives us wonderful images. The words are instantly familiar as heard so often set to music. One theory is that they were enacted at the temple gates as part of the corporate worship. People outside the temple would call out for the gates to be opened so that the King of Glory could come in. The priests inside the temple would ask, 'Who is this King of Glory?' and the people would respond, 'The Lord strong and mighty, the Lord mighty in battle.' The gates would then be opened so that God's presence was with them. It also looked forward to the entry of Christ into the new Jerusalem.

At the beginning of the service to celebrate The Presentation of Christ in the Temple give everyone a candle. Just before the psalm, the minister can ask the congregation to go outside with their unlit candles. The doors of the church are shut. The people outside call out, 'Open the doors so that the King of Glory may come in!' The minister can call out, 'Who is this King of Glory?'. The people answer, 'The Lord Almighty, he is the King of Glory!' The minister opens the doors. The people come back in and as they come in their candles are lit. The candles remain lighted until after the Gospel reading.

It is when Mary and Joseph bring Jesus to the temple that Simeon reveals him as a light for revelation to the Gentiles and for glory to his people Israel.

As has been said earlier in this section Candlemas is the end of the Christmas season. It is now that we leave Christmas behind and turn to Holy Week. One symbolic way of doing this in worship is to place a plain wooden cross by the door and, at the end of the service, ask everyone to turn around and face it during the dismissal.

Putting the Christmas decorations away

There is much scope for symbolism at the end of a Candlemas service. While the congregation are still present, or during coffee time, read Ecclesiastes 3.1–8 out loud. Or play 'Turn! Turn! Turn! – To everything there is a season' a song recorded by the pop group The Byrds in the 1960s based on that Bible reading.

While this is happening ask a small group of people to carefully take down and wrap the Christmas decorations and crib scene. Put them away in a box. Do this in full view of the congregation.

If you have a Christmas tree in church undress it and take it down. Ask an adult in the congregation to supervise the sawing off of all the branches - until just the trunk is left. This can be kept and turned into a cross for Good Friday. So the tree of life becomes the tree of crucifixion. At Easter we will find it once again decorated, this time with flowers, as a tree of resurrection.

These may sound like difficult, painful things to do, but they mark an important turning point in our Christian journey.

Discussion time

Instead of a sermon ask the congregation to form small groups. Mary and Joseph take Jesus to the temple to be presented and consecrated to the Lord and to offer their sacrifice of a pair of doves or two young pigeons. In this Jesus is treated as any other firstborn son. Give the groups the Gospel reading to look at.

Simeon recognizes Jesus and says to Mary, 'The child is destined to cause the falling and rising of many. And a sword will pierce your own soul too'. What do you suppose Mary must have thought? What did Simeon mean? Jesus is to be the 'light for revelation to the Gentiles', and yet Simeon speaks of suffering and pain to come. Mary must have felt a mother's deep sense of fear and foreboding at these words. And Joseph – a saint by all accounts – must wonder what he is caught up in. We read the Gospel story in the knowledge of hindsight. We can only try to imagine how this young couple must have felt. Ask the small groups to have a short discussion.

LENT

Lent, Holy Week and Easter are the seasons that give meaning and truth to the Christian faith. They evoke emotions that draw us down into the depths of darkness and sorrow as we approach and experience the Good Friday liturgy of crucifixion. We are then lifted up to new light and life as we celebrate Easter Day. We live through the weeks of Lent and Holy Week in the knowledge that 'all will, in the end, be well'. Those first disciples of Jesus did not.

Get a group of people together to think about Lent. It may well be that your minister will suggest a Lent book to read. There may be Lent discussion groups in the parish or with Churches Together in the area. These are good things to join. However, the weeks during Lent can also provide an opportunity to draw people together in order to look outwards.

We tend to 'give something up' during Lent. This is a form of fasting and discipline. Lent can also be a time to 'take something on'. It can be a time to 'do' rather than 'be'. A time to face outwards instead of inwards. It can, indeed, be a time of outreach in the life of the Church. It can be a time when we can become 'Christ in the world'.

We give some ideas for Lenten activities using the theme of 'looking outwards' both in our own neighbourhood and in the wider world.

READINGS FOR LENT

Ash Wednesday
Years A, B and C

Joel 2.1–2, 12–17 *or* Isaiah 58.1–12
Psalm 51.1–18
2 Corinthians 5.20b—6.10
Matthew 6.1–6, 16–21 *or* John 8.1–11

Palm Sunday
Year A

Liturgy of the Palms:
Matthew 21.1–11
Psalm 118.1–2, 19–29
Liturgy of the Passion:
Isaiah 50.4–9a
Psalm 31.9–16
Philippians 2.5–11
Matthew 26.14—27.66
   or Matthew 27.11–54

Year B

Liturgy of the Palms:
Mark 11.1–11 *or* John 12.12–16
Psalm 118.1–2, 19–24
Liturgy of the Passion:
Isaiah 50.4–9a
Psalm 31.9–16
Philippians 2.5–11
Mark 14.1—15.47
   or Mark 15.1–39 (40–47)

Year C

Liturgy of the Palms:
Luke 19.28–40
Psalm 118.1–2, 19–29
Liturgy of the Passion:
Isaiah 50.4–9a
Psalm 31.9–16
Philippians 2.5–11
Luke 22.14—23.56 *or* Luke 23.1–49

Maundy Thursday
Years A, B and C

Exodus 12.1–4 (5–10), 11–14
Psalm 116.1, 10–17
1 Corinthians 11.23–26
John 13.1–17, 31b–35

Good Friday
Years A, B and C

Isaiah 52.13—53.12
Psalm 22
Hebrews 10.16–25
   or Hebrews 4.14–16; 5.7–9
John 18.1—19.42

HYMNS AND SONGS FOR LENT AND HOLY WEEK

Details of these hymnbooks and song books are on pages xxi–xxiv.

Be Still and Know

Keep watch with me
O God, you search me

Come All You People

Take, O take me as I am

Common Ground

Tree of Life

Hymns of Glory, Songs of Praise

Ah, holy Jesus, how hast thou offended
Hosanna, loud hosanna
Lay down your head, Lord Jesus Christ
Open are the gifts of God
Ride on, ride on, the time is right

Laudate

Again we keep this solemn fast
Come to Jerusalem
Eye has not seen
Jesus the Lord said: 'I am the bread'
Take this moment
Unless a grain of wheat

Restless Is the Heart

Everyday God

Resurrexit

Adoramus te Christe
Kyrie eleison (Lenten Litany)
This is the wood of the Cross

Songs from Taizé

Eat this bread
Jesus, remember me
O Christe Domine Jesu
Stay with me

The Courage to Say No

O Jesus Christ, in human flesh

The Source

Broken for me
From heaven you came (The Servant King)
How deep the Father's love for us
Lord, I lift your name on high (You came from heaven to earth)
You laid aside your majesty (I really want to worship you, my Lord)

There Is One Among Us

This is the body of Christ

Twenty-First Century Folk Hymnal

O holy, most holy, the God of creation
O Lamb of God

SONG OF PRAYER

Tune: Quem Pastores 88 87

1   As our prayers to you are rising,
    through the Son with you abiding,
    powerful in the Spirit's guiding,
    hold us, gracious Lord, we pray.

2   In our worship and our singing,
    in the praise that we are bringing,
    as together we are seeking,
    hold us, gracious Lord, we pray.

3   In the stories we are hearing,
    in the lessons we are learning,
    in your truth and its unfolding,
    hold us, gracious Lord, we pray.

4   In the bread that we are breaking,
    in the wine that we are sharing,
    in this sacramental feasting,
    hold us, gracious Lord, we pray.

5   In our loving and our living,
    in our taking and our giving,
    in our birthing and our dying,
    hold us, gracious Lord, we pray.

6   In our pain and in our hurting,
    in our grief and in our mourning,
    in the wonder of your healing,
    hold us, gracious Lord, we pray.

7   In our joy and in our laughing,
    in the music of our dancing,
    in the hope of life unending,
    hold us, gracious Lord, we pray.

8   In our waking and our sleeping,
    in our sowing and our reaping,
    in our friendships and their keeping,
    hold us, gracious Lord, we pray.

9   With the saints and their inspiring,
    these our prayers are sung rejoicing,
    in the name of Christ, uniting,
    hold us, gracious Lord, we pray.

© Jan Brind

LITANY FOR LENT

For moonlit nights and sparkling stars
We bless you, Lord.
For blue skies and wind-driven clouds
We bless you, Lord.
For gentle rain and warm sun
We bless you, Lord.
For seeds that stir in the good earth
We bless you, Lord.
For green leaves and fragrant blossom
We bless you, Lord.
For nesting birds and promise of spring
We bless you, Lord.
For creatures great and creatures small
We bless you, Lord.
For families and friends
We bless you, Lord.
For the continuing rhythm of life
We bless you, Lord.

For love embodied in the washing of feet
We thank you, Lord.
For broken bread and wine outpoured
We thank you, Lord.
For the promise of sins forgiven
We thank you, Lord.
For your life laid down for us
We thank you, Lord.
For your rising to new life
We thank you, Lord.
For companions we meet on the way
We thank you, Lord.
For moments of recognition
We thank you, Lord.
For leaving us your peace
We thank you, Lord.
For the gift of your Holy Spirit
We thank you, Lord.

That justice and mercy may prevail
We pray to you, Lord.
That the earth's resources may be shared equally
We pray to you, Lord.
That the hungry may be fed
We pray to you, Lord.
That the sick may be healed
We pray to you, Lord.
That the homeless may find shelter
We pray to you, Lord.
That the frightened may know your presence
We pray to you, Lord.
That the lonely may be comforted
We pray to you, Lord.
That the dying may be filled with your peace
We pray to you, Lord.
That we may follow in the footsteps of the saints
We pray to you, Lord.

In times of wilderness and waiting
Be near us, Good Lord.
In times of searching and questioning
Be near us, Good Lord.
In times of praying and silence
Be near us, Good Lord.
In times when our faith is unsure
Be near us, Good Lord.
In speaking your words of love to others
Be near us, Good Lord.
In serving our brothers and sisters in your name
Be near us, Good Lord.
In taking up what burdens us
Be near us, Good Lord.
In striving to be your disciples
Be near us, Good Lord.
In the hope of rising to new life in you
Be near us, Good Lord.

PALMS, BANNERS AND STOLES FOR PALM SUNDAY

Because Palm Sunday is part of the Lent season the church is often only decorated with green palms – something quick to put up and take down again. It is a time of year when everyone is extremely busy and having time to plan and decorate for another event may be one thing too many. If there is time, some simple banners or stoles could be made during Lent, before the big build up to Holy Week and Easter begins.

Paper banners

Make simple paper banners using words such as 'Hosanna' or 'King of Kings' or 'Ride on, ride on in majesty'. Hang these around the church or down the pillars.

Stoles

Stoles can be made with similar words on. The letters to be sprayed over can be cut out in paper and stuck on the stole. A stencil in the shape of a palm can be cut out and sprayed through over the letters. The stencil and paper letters are then removed and the stole is made up.

BANNERS AND ALTAR FRONTALS FOR
LENT AND HOLY WEEK

Lent is a season when we are encouraged to look at ourselves and see where we might make some improvements in our lives. The banners or altar frontals used in church can help us to reflect on what we get wrong and, therefore, what we would like to put right. It is a time to be aware of the amazing forgiveness that God offers whenever we ask for it.

The Passion story gives us such a vivid and real account of what happened during the last days of Jesus' life and how people behaved. They betrayed him, they ran away, they denied they knew him, they washed their hands, they doubted – in fact they behaved like regular human beings. They behaved like us.

Put words on the banners or altar frontals that both acknowledge our failings, but that also offer us the ever-present hope of God's forgiveness.

Father forgive 'nails'

Make 'nails' out of paper. Put words on them that reflect the failing of the disciples and others during the Passion story: 'betrayed with a kiss', 'watch and pray', 'before the cock crows twice', 'I do not know the man', 'crucify him' – the list is endless. Then make the paper nails into the words 'Father Forgive'. If a computer is available the *WordArt Gallery* offers designs for letters to go both horizontally and vertically. Then the words can be written along or down the 'nail'.

Father forgive nail cross

Or do the reverse to the above. Make very large paper nails with 'Father forgive' written on them, and then make the nails into a cross.

CRUCIFY HIM

I DO NOT KNOW THE MAN

FATHER FORGIVE

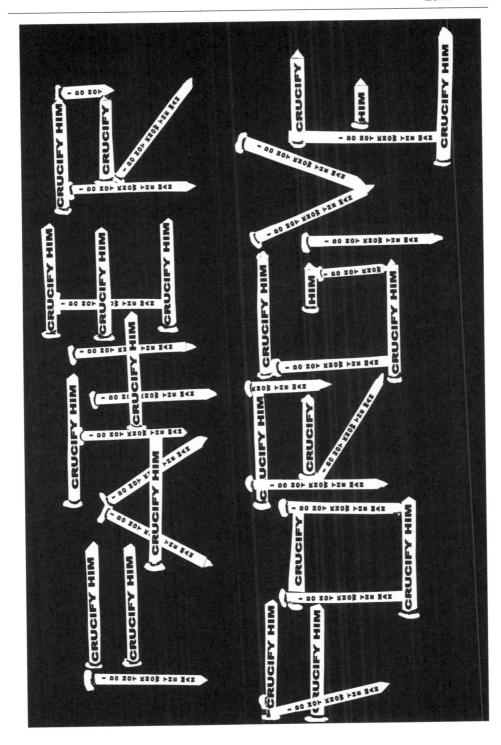

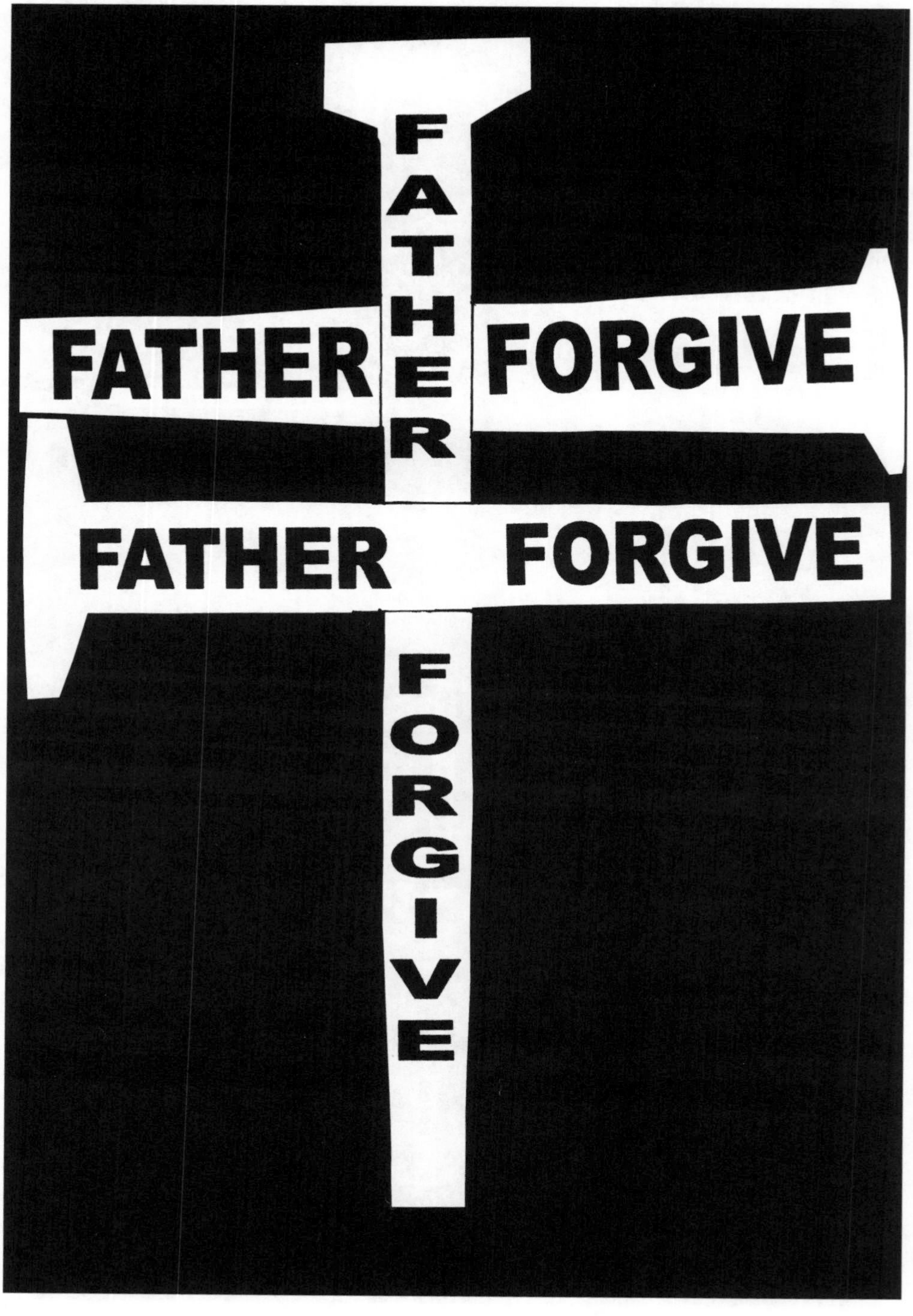
FATHER
FATHER FORGIVE
FATHER FORGIVE
FORGIVE

Forgive us 'stones'

Cut out paper stones and use these to write 'Forgive us', or 'Has no one condemned you?' It is in John's Gospel that the story of the woman caught in adultery is told. Jesus asks 'whichever one of you has committed no sin may throw the first stone'. These words remind us that God forgives us and we need to forgive each other. The paper stones can be cut out of wallpaper with a 'stone' pattern on it. Often in wallpaper shops it is possible to buy odd rolls of wallpaper or 'borders'. These are ideal for cutting out stone shapes. After sticking the stones onto the background add some shading so the stones look as if they stand off the paper.

PARISH ACTIVITIES FOR LENT

Themes for each week of Lent

Each of the five Sundays in Lent can have a special focus.

Choose five places in the church where you can set up a prayer station. Place a candle in each place, and words and pictures to describe the station. During the five weeks you can, in turn, look at family issues, community issues, local issues, national issues and global issues. Each Sunday introduce the following week's focus and light the candle. Invite speakers to come midweek and talk about specific subjects related to that week's focus – local prison, community mental health centre, drug rehabilitation, recycling, hostel, homeless, school exclusion, fair trade, racial justice. The list is endless. On the following Sunday ask several of the people who attended the talk to share with the congregation what they learned. Then light the next candle.

Christian speakers from churches overseas

Have five 'country' prayer stations in church. Place candles and pictures describing the country in each station. On each of the five Sundays invite Christians from those countries to come and talk about their church at home and their faith. Light the appropriate candle and offer prayers for the people and mission of that country.

Picking things up to carry in Lent

Sometimes we can be helped to focus on Lent if we have something to carry with us. This can be something we can touch in our pocket to remind us that it is Lent. It can help to bring us closer to God and be a reminder that God is there with us at all times. On the first Sunday in Lent there can be a basket placed somewhere in church. Place a selection of the following items in the basket – small nails, stones, small wooden crosses, or 'holding' crosses. Each person can be encouraged to choose an item to keep close to them during the 40 days of Lent. At the end of Lent the items can be placed back in the basket to mark the ending of Lent. If a nail has been carried it can be placed at the foot of the cross on Good Friday, or it can be hammered into the cross as a way of acknowledging our responsibility for the sin of the world – but also as a symbol of God's love and forgiveness.

Lent cards

Lent is often used by people as a time to 'give something up' or to 'take something up'. It is a very neat 40 days with a clear beginning and end and often people feel able to commit themselves to something during that time. To help everyone make a commitment for those 40 days each member of the congregation can be given a card and envelope sometime during the service on the first Sunday in Lent. They should be encouraged to use the cards to help them reflect on what they might 'put down' or 'take up' during the 40 days. There is a wonderful reading from Isaiah 58 telling us what God wants from a fast. This could be printed on the front of the card. On the back of the card everyone writes what they are going to 'do' or 'not do' during Lent. They put the card in a sealed envelope – only they know what is written on the card. Each person keeps their card sealed in the envelope somewhere safe during Lent and then, at the end of Lent, all the cards can be disposed of in a symbolic manner. They can either be burned on the Easter Saturday

---

THIS IS THE KIND OF FAST DAY I'M AFTER

Break the chains of injustice,
Get rid of exploitation in the work place,
Free the oppressed,
Cancel debts.

What I am interested in seeing you do is:
Sharing your food with the hungry,
Inviting the homeless poor into your homes,
Putting clothes on the shivering ill-clad,
Being available to your own families.

Do this and the lights will turn on
and your life will turn around at once.
Your righteousness will pave your way.
The God of Glory will secure your passage.
Then when you pray, God will answer.
You'll call out for help and I'll say,
'Here I am'.

Words from Isaiah 58, taken from *The Message* by E. Peterson

vigil bonfire, or they can be burned in a bowl using the flame from the newly lit Paschal Candle. Alternatively, the cards can be placed in a collection basket on Easter Day and then placed on the altar, so acknowledging the end of Lent, and offering to God what has been done during this time.

Justice meal 'fasting or feasting'

Find out the ratio of 'western well fed' to 'third world starving'. There are plenty of web sites you can visit – try those concerned with poverty, fair trade and trade justice, for example Christian Aid and Cafod. Organize a parish meal. Everyone buys a ticket. Before the meal is served ask everyone to put their tickets in a hat. Draw out the number of 'well fed' people who will be given a good meal. The rest receive rice. How does it feel to only have rice when your neighbour is eating a feast? Or how does it feel to be feasting when all around you are eating rice? Invite a speaker to come – many of the above organizations have local reps who are only too pleased to be asked.

Palm Sunday

As well as the small palms that we receive on Palm Sunday use large ever-green branches to wave. See if you can borrow a real donkey for the main service. Starting outside the church, process to the church door behind the donkey singing one of the Hosanna songs. Many donkeys are happy to come right into the building – and some are not! Please don't frighten the donkey by insisting he enters the church – play it by ear! By the time everyone is in church the singing will be wonderfully out of time but this just adds to the excitement!

Maundy Thursday night watch

Before the Maundy Thursday service create a Garden of Gethsemane in the church. This can be done using boxes of different shapes and sizes. Drape green material over them. Arrange candles in night lights and pots of primroses and greenery. You can also place symbolic signs in among the candles – a goblet lying on its side, bread crumbs, a handful of coins spilling out of a bag, a small sword and a cockerel. Place rugs and stools on the floor and chairs in a circle. Leave some Bibles and Lent books for people to look at. As the Maundy Thursday service ends light the candles and dim the lights. It is a good idea to have a roster of watchers so that there are always at least two people watching together. Towards midnight quietly sing songs from the Taizé community.

Good Friday walk of witness

Find out if there is a local Churches Together walk of witness and outdoor service near you. Organize a group from the church to walk together.

Good Friday

If you have a Sunday School invite the children and helpers and families to a morning of themed games and drama. Organize a treasure hunt. End the morning by sharing hot cross buns and hot and cold drinks together.

The wooden cross

Many people erect a simple, stark, wooden cross in church on Good Friday. If you cut down your Christmas tree at the end of Christmas or Epiphany, and kept the trunk, this can be made into the Good Friday cross. Use the same piece of wood to celebrate Christmas, Good Friday and Easter Day – birth and death and new life.

Mothering Sunday

Mothering Sunday in the UK falls during the season of Lent. Sometimes called 'Refreshment Sunday' it used to be the day when girls in service were allowed home to visit their families. Simnel cake was eaten. Today we are more likely to eat Simnel cake on Easter Day. (See the recipe for this in the Easter section on p. 138.) Mothering Sunday is a feast day that draws many people to church who might not normally attend. It is a time to celebrate 'family' and give thanks for all mothers, past and present. The Bible readings focus on the mothers of Moses, Samuel and Jesus. It is a time, too, when we remember our cathedral church and its role as 'mother church' to the churches in the diocese. The people in our church communities make up the family of the Church. We are all part of this family and should care for one another. Maybe this makes it a little easier to understand Jesus' last words to his mother and to the disciple whom he loved: *He said to his mother, 'Dear woman, here is your son', and to the disciple, 'Here is your mother.'* John 19.26–27

READINGS FOR MOTHERING SUNDAY

Years A, B and C

Exodus 2.1–10 *or* 1 Samuel 1.20–28
Psalm 34.11–20 *or* Psalm 127.1–4
2 Corinthians 1.3–7 *or* Colossians 3.12–17
Luke 2.33–35 *or* John 19.25–27

HYMNS AND SONGS FOR MOTHERING SUNDAY

Details of these hymn books and song books are on pages xxi–xxiv.

Be Still and Know

    Like a child rests
    Magnificat
    O God, you search me

Hymns Old and New: New Anglican Edition

    For Mary, mother of our Lord
    For the beauty of the earth
    Let there be love
    Lord, we come to ask your healing
    Make me a channel of your peace
    Now thank we all our God

Innkeepers and Light Sleepers

    No wind at the window

Laudate

    Holy is his name
    My soul proclaims you, mighty God
    Our Father, by whose name

PRAYERS FOR MOTHERING SUNDAY

Let us be still, and draw close to the presence of God, as we offer our prayers in faith.

Heavenly Father, we are all children in your family and you have created us to live in harmony. We pray for the Church worldwide that there may be a greater understanding between those of different cultures and traditions. Guide us and direct all our thoughts so that our hearts may be full of trust and acceptance as we grow ever more closely together.
God of compassion,
Fill us with your love.

We pray for our cathedral church as she watches over our diocese. May we be mindful of the leadership and example that she sets. We pray for our sister churches that we may increasingly find ways to interact and share fellowship. We pray that together we may bring the good news to all those whose spirits are in need of refreshment.
God of compassion,
Fill us with your love.

Today we give special thanks for our mothers and for their love and care so freely given. We remember our grandmothers and our godmothers and all those who have fulfilled maternal roles in our lives. May they be blessed with the knowledge that being a mother can bring pain as well as joy and that, as with the mothers of Moses, Samuel and Jesus, there must be a loving and a letting go.
God of compassion,
Fill us with your love.

We pray for those among us who suffer in body, mind or spirit. May we reach out to them as you reach out to us. May we care for each other as members of one family. We remember those who have gone before us and who now rest with you in heaven. Bring comfort to those for whom this day brings difficulty and sorrow.
God of compassion,
Fill us with your love.

Heavenly Father, you patiently watch over your children offering guidance to those who seek, strength to those who falter, and forgiveness to those who sin. Hear us, gracious Lord, as we offer these prayers to you.
Amen

BANNERS AND ALTAR FRONTALS
FOR MOTHERING SUNDAY

Paper banner or altar frontal

Before Mothering Sunday ask the Sunday School or children in the congregation to paint pictures of their mothers or someone whom they love. Cut round each one and stick onto a paper background. You can write 'God bless our mothers' or 'We are God's family' either across the centre or around the edge.

PARISH ACTIVITIES FOR MOTHERING SUNDAY

An exercise to do in church on Mothering Sunday using the Gospel reading from John 19.25–27:

So he said to his mother, 'He is your son.' Then he said to the disciple, 'She is your mother.' From that time the disciple took her to live in his home.

The Gospel reading tells of the time when Jesus was dying on the cross. Despite the pain and the anguish that he must have been experiencing he still managed to show love and concern for those standing at the foot of the cross watching him die. How often, in our busy lives, do we think, 'Oh, I must get in touch with so and so' and yet we never do? Here is an extraordinary example of responding to a perceived need. Jesus was aware that his mother would be alone, and would need looking after. He responded immediately, in spite of being in such agony, and asked his dear friend John to look after his mother. We often need to be reminded that we are all part of God's family, and if a family really works the members need to look out for one another. Just as Jesus did in the last moments of his life.

- Ask the congregation to imagine that they are standing at the foot of the cross.
- The entire congregation is there, old and young, happy and sad.
- Ask them to think whom it would be that Jesus would tell them they were linked to, whom should they be looking after, inviting home for a cup of tea, making friends with, or going to the pub with?
- Who are their mothers, sons, daughters, fathers, aunts, uncles or friends?
- Challenge them to respond to that calling during the second part of Lent.
- On Easter Day ask for volunteers to tell the congregation what came from that challenge and what new links may have been forged.

Cards to give out on Mothering Sunday

Colossians 3.12–17

Therefore, as God's chosen people, holy and dearly loved, clothe yourselves with compassion, kindness, humility, gentleness and patience.

This is a beautiful passage from Colossians. Think what it would be like to be literally clothed in these gifts. Make cards to hand to everyone on Mothering Sunday. Draw a person and a full set of clothing on each card. Each article of clothing can have the name of one of the gifts mentioned in this passage. Draw tabs on the clothing. Let everyone take a card home.

Biscuits

It is traditional in most churches for children to present posies of flowers to their mothers and all the women in the congregation on Mothering Sunday. Heart-shaped biscuits can also be made and handed to people as they leave church. (See the recipe following.) Wrap them up in cellophane tied with a ribbon. Attach a tag to each one and write 'With love from the family of the church'. Make enough biscuits to distribute to neighbours in the community. Take the love of Christ out from the church to those who live nearby.

HEART-SHAPED BISCUITS

You will need heart-shaped biscuit cutters

Oven temperature: 350°F, 180°C, gas mark 4

Ingredients:

100g (4oz) butter or margarine
100g (4oz) caster sugar
1 egg, beaten
200g (8oz) flour
(Icing sugar and pink food colouring for glacé icing)

Method:

Grease two baking trays. Cream the butter and sugar until pale and fluffy. Add the egg a little at a time, beating after each addition. Stir in the flour and mix to a fairly firm dough. Knead lightly and roll out 0.5cm (¼ inch) thick on a floured board. Carefully cut heart shapes with the biscuit cutter. Lift onto a greased tray and bake in the top of the oven for 15–20 minutes until firm and very lightly browned. Leave on the trays to cool for a few minutes before transferring to wire racks. The biscuits can be iced with pink glacé icing if you wish and decorated.
   This makes about 20 biscuits.

EASTER

The light of Christ.
Thanks be to God!

Easter Day has dawned and for some it will have dawned very early with a dawn service. The new Paschal Candle will have been lit casting a mellow glow around a church that is still in shadow. The people may each have a lighted candle lit from the Christ Light. There may be a simple breakfast in church. It is a time when the world seems new and exciting and somehow nothing will ever be the same again. The disciples must surely have felt this when they first saw Jesus face to face after his resurrection.

We give ideas here for reviving the tree that has journeyed so far – Christmas to Good Friday to Easter Day. Churches can be decorated with flowers and butterflies and, of course, chocolate eggs.

Easter Day

READINGS FOR EASTER

Year A

Acts 10.34–43 *or* Jeremiah 31.1–6
Psalm 118.1–2, 14–24
Colossians 3.1–4 *or* Acts 10.34–43
John 20.1–18 *or* Matthew 28.1–10

Year B

Acts 10.34–43 *or* Isaiah 25.6–9
Psalm 118.1–2, 14–24
1 Corinthians 15.1–11 *or* Acts 10.34–43
John 20.1–18 *or* Mark 16.1–8

Year C

Acts 10.34–43 *or* Isaiah 65.17–25
Psalm 118.1–2, 14–24
1 Corinthians 15.19–26 *or* Acts 10.34–43
John 20.1–18 *or* Luke 24.1–12

HYMNS AND SONGS FOR EASTER

Details of these hymn books and song books are on pages xxi–xxiv.

Be Still and Know

Going home

Go Before Us

Alleluia! Raise the Gospel

Hymns of Glory, Songs of Praise

Christ has risen while earth slumbers
Jesus is risen, alleluia!
This joyful Eastertide
Word of the Father (Eastertide Acclamation)

Hymns Old & New: One Church, One Faith, One Lord

Alleluia, alleluia, hearts to heaven and voices raise
Before the throne
In Christ alone

Laudate

Easter Alleluia
He is risen, tell the story
On the journey to Emmaus
Thanks be to God
The stone that the builders rejected
Unless a grain of wheat
We walk by faith

Resurrexit

Bright morning
Christ, be our light
We gathered there
Word that formed creation

Share the Light

The peace of God

Sing Glory

All shall be well
Alleluia, alleluia, Jesus, Risen Lord of Life
If Christ had not been raised from death
Jesus, Prince and Saviour

Songs from Taizé

Jesus, the Lord, is risen (Surrexit Dominus vere – Canon)
The Lord is risen (Surrexit Christus)

Songs of Fellowship

I am the bread of life

The Source

All heaven declares
He has risen
I will offer up my life (This thankful heart)
Jesus Christ (Once again)
Jesus, Jesus (Holy and anointed one)
Overwhelmed by love

EASTER HYMN

Tune: Londonderry Air 11 10 11 10 11 10 11 12

1   Christ is alive! the new day dawns with promise;
    An empty tomb, the stone is rolled away;
    With life renewed, the flame is burning brightly;
    The light of love has overcome the grave.
    Sing alleluia, Christ is truly risen!
    Sing alleluia, Christ is truly here!
    Christ is alive! the new day dawns with promise;
    Sing alleluia, Christ the risen Lord is here!

2   Christ is the Way, and we must surely follow;
    Through sun and storm he'll call us to his side
    To be as one, and joined with all creation,
    We'll work for peace to make his kingdom come.
    Sing alleluia, Christ is truly risen!
    Sing alleluia, Christ is truly here!
    Christ is the Way, and we must surely follow;
    Sing alleluia, Christ the risen Lord is here!

3   Christ is the Truth, and we must seek no other;
    His words of love will keep us ever near;
    We'll see his face in every friend and stranger;
    His healing touch to soothe away our fear.
    Sing alleluia, Christ is truly risen!
    Sing alleluia, Christ is truly here!
    Christ is the Truth, and we must seek no other;
    Sing alleluia, Christ the risen Lord is here!

4   Christis the Life, and we must live it fully;
    We'll share his cup and eat his living bread;
    As he has loved so we must love each other,
    So all the world will know we are his friends.
    Sing alleluia, Christ is truly risen!
    Sing alleluia, Christ is truly here!
    Christ is the Life, and we must live it fully;
    Sing alleluia, Christ the risen Lord is here!

© Jan Brind

PRAYERS FOR THE ROAD TO EMMAUS

Risen Lord, we gather together in this place of prayer to worship you in song and in silence. We give thanks for the companionship we find and for the chance to walk together for a while in your company.
We pray to you, Lord.
Lord, hear our prayer.

Risen Lord, help us to listen to you so that, like the two disciples on the Road to Emmaus, our hearts may burn within us and we may recognize your truth.
We pray to you, Lord.
Lord, hear our prayer.

Risen Lord, we pray for your church in this place, and all churches where people gather in your Name. May they continue to be sources of refreshment for all who are drawn to them.
We pray to you, Lord.
Lord, hear our prayer.

Risen Lord, we pray for the troubled places in your world. Where there is fear and darkness may you bring peace and light. May those in positions of trust and authority recognize you walking beside them showing the way.
We pray to you, Lord.
Lord, hear our prayer.

Risen Lord, we pray for those who are sick in body, mind or spirit. In a moment of quiet we remember those dear to us who suffer. (Pause) May we find ways of reaching out in love to those in need.
We pray to you, Lord.
Lord, hear our prayer.

Risen Lord, we know that whenever there is bread to be broken and a story to be told, you are there in the midst of us. As the disciples recognized you in the breaking of bread, we pray that we too may have moments of clarity when our eyes and hearts are opened to your presence.
We pray to you, Lord, and ask you hear our prayer.
Amen

BANNERS AND ALTAR FRONTALS FOR EASTER

Using Words

Print words linked to Easter Day onto banners and altar frontals: Alleluia, He is Risen, Christ is Risen, Peace Be With You, or Then They Were Glad.

Using plain coloured fabric

Plain coloured fabric banners hanging down the pillars or the walls of the church can be very effective. These can be cream, yellow or orange. Start with darker colours at the back of the church and gradually introduce lighter colours as you come forwards – finally using white or gold by the altar.

Using hand shapes

A very effective way of showing 'The Light of the Risen Lord' coming out of the tomb is by using hand shapes. These can be drawn on paper and cut out.

   Or ask people to make hand prints. The smaller members of the congregation will love getting their hands covered in paint. The colour should go from white at the mouth of the tomb, through yellow, orange and finally red. One of the short Easter phrases can be added.

TRANSFORMING THE CHRISTMAS TREE FOR EASTER DAY

Having stripped the Christmas tree of its branches and turned the trunk into a cross for Lent and Holy Week it is important that the 'Christmas tree cross' is decorated again for Easter – so that the tree is once again the centre of celebration.

The symbols that are put on the tree should reflect resurrection and the 'new hope' given to us by Jesus through his death and resurrection. These can be:

- Butterflies: the butterfly breaks out of the chrysalis (the tomb) into new life.
- Flowers: the flower comes out of the ground into the glorious light of day.
- Ribbons: these are often used today as a symbol of welcome, especially yellow ribbon. 'Welcoming Home' – Jesus is welcomed home to be with his Father.
- Hearts: Jesus showed us what true love is by dying on the cross for us.

Each person in the church can decorate a symbol and place it on the tree cross, so transforming it from a thing of torture to a symbol of resurrection. The decoration can happen on Easter Saturday when the church is being decorated for Easter. Maybe the children in the church can decorate the symbols on the Sundays leading up to Easter Day and they can be responsible for the transformation of the 'tree cross'.

Butterflies

1   Fold a piece of paper in half. Draw the shape of half a butterfly on one half. Cut out and open up. The butterfly will have matching shaped wings.

2   Decorate the butterfly:

   • With crayon, felt pen or painted patterns.

   • With self-adhesive sticky spots and stars. Small children love using these.

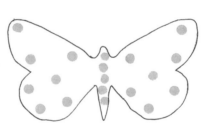

   • With paint. Fold a sheet of paper in half. Open it up again and paint on one side with fairly wet paint. Refold the paper so that the wet paint goes onto the clean half. Open up and allow to dry. When dry cut out in the shape of a butterfly.

   • With carrot spots. Cut a carrot in half. Dip the cut end in some paint and use it to print spots on the cut out butterfly shape.

   • Use a stencil to decorate the cut butterfly shape.

   • Cut out the butterfly shape and then fold the shape again and cut some more shapes out of the wings. These shapes can be fish, crosses and other Christian symbols. This is like a butterfly doily.

Flowers

The flowers can be made from paper, crêpe, tissue or card. Either cut out a simple flower shape in one piece of paper, or cut out petals and stick them onto a central round shape. Or decorate the 'tree cross' with real flowers. Either fix some oasis onto the trunk and arrange the flowers in this, or just tie the flowers on before the Sunday morning service.

FLOWERS

Traditionally, flowers are used to decorate the church at Easter time. They are a strong symbol of resurrection, especially as Easter comes in the spring in the northern hemisphere. The arrival of the first flower, breaking through the winter darkness, is always seen as a herald to the coming of spring and new birth.

Before purchasing the flowers get the flower arrangers together and make a plan. The flowers will have a far greater impact if they are colour co-ordinated. Traditionally the colour used for celebration in the Church is white; to this can be added yellows and light oranges. If different people arrange the flowers let them all know what the colour scheme is to be.

If there are to be arrangements throughout the church building think about a scheme that runs from the back to the altar. At the back there can be dark oranges, reds and yellows. As the arrangements progress through the church towards the altar the colours can gradually change to lighter oranges and yellows, and at the altar there can be light yellows, creams and white. These flowers can reflect the colours of the rising sun. If the church has pillars use plain fabric to hang down them in the same colours as the flowers. The flowers and the fabric will re-enforce the theme of the rising sun.

Find out if the church is going to be decorated with banners or an altar frontal and see if the flowers can link in with them. The shape of the arrangement can be designed to fit with the shape of the design on the frontal.

If your church does not have much money for flowers try to access a source of greenery. If the general shape of the arrangement is made in greenery the numbers of flowers needed is greatly reduced. Artificial flowers used with real flowers and greenery can be very effective. Collect some artificial flowers, but always make sure you use them in season. Daffodils in mid-summer will stand out like a sore thumb, but used in the spring will look entirely in place.

Always remember that garden flowers can be very effective and cost nothing. 'Wild' flowers can also be very effective. Cow parsley, buttercups and daisies can make a wonderful display, but always check that you are allowed to pick them.

   It can be fun to put some Easter symbols in the flower arrangements. It is possible to buy plastic eggs, which look very realistic. These can be put onto a stick and put in the arrangements. If plastic eggs are not available use chicken eggs. It is not difficult to blow them. They can also be fixed onto a stick if a small hole is made in the top. Butterflies fixed onto sticks can also be very effective. There are some very beautiful ones made from feathers that are available in the shops.

Paschal Candle

Using the same colour scheme decorate the Paschal Candle with flowers. The lighting of the new Paschal Candle is an important symbolic moment in the church calendar. Alleluia. Christ is risen! He is risen indeed. Alleluia!

EASTER NESTS

You will need paper cases

Ingredients:

   200g (8oz) chocolate
   150g (6oz) shredded wheat cereal
   mini chocolate eggs

Method:

Break the chocolate into small pieces and place in a dish over a pan of boiling water. Stir until melted. Crumble the shredded wheat and stir into the chocolate. Place spoonfuls into paper cases and make a small indentation in the top of each one. Leave to cool. Place one or two eggs inside each nest.
   This makes about 20 nests.

SIMNEL CAKE

SimNel Cake was traditionally baked on Mothering Sunday. Now it is more usual to eat it on Easter Day. Legend has it that a brother and sister (Simon and Nell) were going to make a cake for their mother. They could not agree on the method of cooking – whether to bake or boil – so they compromised by baking one half and boiling the other. The two cakes were stuck together – hence SimNel Cake! This recipe is for a small 18cm (7 in) cake tin. Increase the quantities for a larger cake.

Oven temperature: 300°F, 150°C, gas mark 2

Ingredients:

175g (6oz) softened butter
175g (6oz) soft dark brown sugar
3 eggs
175g (6oz) plain flour
3 teaspoons mixed spice
1 teaspoon baking powder
2 tablespoons milk
275g (10oz) mixed dried fruit
50g (2oz) chopped glacé cherries

25g (1oz) chopped citrus peel
Grated rind of one lemon
50g (2oz) ground almonds

For decoration

450g (1lb) bought almond paste
1 tablespoon sieved apricot jam
Small wrapped chocolate
    Easter eggs

Method:

Grease and line the baking tin with greased baking parchment. Place all the cake ingredients together in a large bowl and stir until well mixed. Spoon half the mixture into the tin and smooth the top. Divide the bought almond paste into thirds. Roll one third the same size as the baking tin and place on top of the mixture. Put remaining mixture on top of the almond paste. Bake in a cool oven for 2½ hours or until done – test with a skewer. Allow the cake to cool in the tin. Brush the top of the cake with apricot jam. Roll out another third of the almond paste into a circle to fit the top of the cake. With the remaining paste make 11 small balls and place them around the edge. Brush the cake with any remaining jam and brown gently under the grill. When the cake is cool place small wrapped chocolate eggs in the middle.

PARISH ACTIVITIES FOR EASTER

Easter Garden

Easter Saturday is the time to create an Easter Garden in the church ready for Easter Day. It may be something that Sunday School children have prepared in advance or it may be a chance to gather a small working party together. You will need to create a 'tomb' – papier maché stuck onto boxes is good for this. Find a round stone which can be placed next to the entrance as though it has been rolled away. Use your imagination with flowers. There can be three crosses on a raised area. The garden can be any size.

Easter morning egg hunt

Have you ever searched for little eggs in the church on Easter morning? These can be placed all around the church in nooks and crannies where they can be seen easily. After the service, while coffee and cake are being served, children can collect the eggs.

Pentecost

When we think of Pentecost we very often picture a dove in our minds. In fact, no doves are mentioned in the reading from Acts describing the Day of Pentecost. It is elsewhere in the Bible that the Holy Spirit is described as a dove – in Genesis the Spirit of God 'hovers' over the waters; and when Jesus is baptized by John the Spirit descends on him 'like a dove'.

When the believers gather in Jerusalem at Pentecost, 50 days after the Passover, the Holy Spirit does not come as a gentle dove but comes instead with power – in 'tongues of flame' and in a 'strong wind'. As the season of Pentecost falls during the summer months it is a perfect time to plan a special outdoor event. A marquee set up on a village green, or a public hall in the middle of the community, can become the perfect place to celebrate the coming of the Holy Spirit. Be creative! Take 'church' out of the church building and invite everyone to a special service. Decorate the marquee or hall with banners, ribbons, balloons and flowers using Holy Spirit colours of red and yellow and orange. Invite people to bring a picnic to share after the service.

There are ideas in this chapter to help you decorate your worship space for Pentecost. There are ideas for workshops using the themes of language and gift. Maybe now is the time to look at everyone's gifts and see how the body of Christ manifests itself in your community. You may be surprised at the creativity and fruitfulness of the Holy Spirit in your midst!

READINGS FOR THE DAY OF PENTECOST

The reading from Acts must be used as either the first or second reading.

Year A

Acts 2.1–21 *or* Numbers 11.24–30
Psalm 104.26–36, 37b
1 Corinthians 12.3b–13 *or* Acts 2.1–21
John 20.19–23 *or* John 7.37–39

Year B

Acts 2.1–21 *or* Ezekiel 37.1–14
Psalm 104.26–36, 37b
Romans 8.22–27 *or* Acts 2.1–21
John 15.26–27 and 16.4b–15

Year C

Acts 2.1–21 *or* Genesis 11.1–9
Psalm 104.26–36, 37b
Romans 8.14–17 *or* Acts 2.1–21
John 14.8–17 (25–27)

HYMNS AND SONGS FOR PENTECOST

Details of these hymn books and songbooks are on pages xxi–xxiv.

Be Still and Know

Veni lumen cordium

Common Ground

Spirit of God, unseen as the wind
Like the murmur of the dove's song

Enemy of Apathy

Enemy of apathy
Heaven on earth

Go Before Us

Christ beside us

Hymns of Glory, Songs of Praise

Come, Holy Spirit, come!
Holy Spirit, ever living
Holy Spirit, gift bestower
Lord, you sometimes speak in wonders
Loving Spirit, loving Spirit
Spirit of love, you move within creation
We sing a love that sets all people free

Hymns Old and New: New Anglican Edition

A new commandment
Let there be love
Let us talents and tongues employ
Spirit of the living God
The Spirit lives to set us free

Hymns Old & New: One Church, One Faith, One Lord

God forgave my sin (Freely, freely)
God is here! As we his people
Here in this place (Gather us in)
Lord, you created a world full of splendour
O Breath of Life, come sweeping through us

Laudate

Father, Lord of earth and heaven

Songs of Fellowship

Lord, the light of your love is shining
Wind, wind blow on me

Share the Light

Share the light

Sing Glory

Born by the Holy Spirit's breath
Spirit of holiness, wisdom and faithfulness
The Spirit came as promised

Songs from Taizé

Ubi caritas
Veni Sancte Spiritus

The Source

All to Jesus I surrender (I surrender all)
Be still, for the presence of the Lord
I am a new creation
Jesus, Jesus (Holy and anointed one)
Lord, I come to you (The power of your love)
Over the mountains and the sea (I could sing of your love for ever)
Teach me to dance

PENTECOST HYMN

Tune: All through the night 84 84 88 84

1   Holy Spirit, come among us,
    gentle as love;
    bring your healing presence to us,
    peace from above:
    in your troubled world divided,
    let your people now be guided,
    Holy Spirit, come among us,
    gentle as love.

2   Holy Spirit, move about us,
    calm in the storm;
    free our inhibitions from us,
    life to transform:
    when our hearts are bruised and silent,
    fruitful gifts will make them vibrant,
    Holy Spirit, move about us,
    calm in the storm.

3   Holy Spirit, shine within us,
    bright as a flame;
    burn the darkest shadows from us,
    light to proclaim:
    where your people live in sadness,
    you will bring both hope and gladness,
    Holy Spirit, shine within us,
    bright as a flame.

© Jan Brind

CHILDREN'S PENTECOST SONG

Tune: The Grand Old Duke of York

1   Oh, the Holy Spirit came
with tongues of fire and flame,
with rushing wind and wondrous power
the Holy Spirit came.

And when the people spoke,
and danced and clapped their hands,
they found that they could understand
their friends from other lands!

2   Oh, the Holy Spirit comes
with tongues of wind and flame,
with rushing wind and wondrous power
She'll fill us once again!

And when we sing this song,
and dance and clap our hands,
we'll feel God's love and joy and peace
fulfilling God's own plan.

© Jan Brind

PRAYERS FOR PENTECOST

Intercessions

We pray for the life of this church and for all the people who have come together today to sing your praises:
Creator God,
Fill us with your spirit.

We pray for your Church throughout the world and for those who bring us the good news of Jesus Christ:
Creator God,
Fill us with your spirit.

We pray for peace in the troubled places of your world, in particular . . . :
Creator God,
Fill us with your spirit.

We pray for your creation. Help us to look after the beautiful things that are around us and to share them equally with our neighbours:
Creator God
Fill us with your spirit.

We pray for all people who are sick or afraid. Today we hold up to you . . . Help us to care for them:
Creator God,
Fill us with your spirit.

We pray for our families and friends and all whom we love:
Creator God,
Fill us with your spirit.

We offer all these prayers to you, Creator God, asking that you will fill us with your Holy Spirit.
Amen

Or

For the Church of Christ in this place, for our bishops and priests
and all who inspire us with the good news of *love* and *joy* and *peace*:
We pray,
Come, Holy Spirit.

For those who hold positions of authority and power, for the government and
those who serve, that they may hold *faithfully* to what is true and just:
We pray,
Come, Holy Spirit.

For the hurting and dark places of your world where there is conflict and
oppression, in particular ... , that there may be peace and *self-control*:
We pray,
Come, Holy Spirit.

For the peoples of the world who are hungry, that we who have so much may
kindle a spirit of *generosity*:
We pray,
Come, Holy Spirit.

For those who suffer in mind, body or spirit, that we may show *patience,
kindness* and *gentleness*:
We pray,
Come, Holy Spirit.

For those who have died, that they may find everlasting joy in heaven, and for
those who mourn their loss:
We pray,
Come, Holy Spirit.

For our families and neighbours and ourselves, that we may show forth the
fruit of your Holy Spirit in our daily lives:
We pray,
Come, Holy Spirit.

Or

Lord of wind and flame, fill us with the breath of your Spirit and the fire of your love:
We pray to you.
Lord, have mercy.

Lord of hopes and dreams, give us the vision to realize your kingdom here on earth:
We pray to you.
Lord, have mercy.

Lord of heaven and earth, help us to recognize the wonders that are around us:
We pray to you.
Lord, have mercy.

Lord of all eternity, have mercy on us and bless us:
We pray to you.
Lord, have mercy.

WORKSHOP ACTIVITY USING
PLACES AND LANGUAGES

Plan a workshop to look at and explore the places named in the Pentecost story in Acts 2: Parthia, Media, Elam, Mesopotamia, Judaea, Cappadocia, Pontus, Asia, Phrygia, Pamphylia, Egypt, Libya, Cyrene, Rome, Crete, Arabia. How many times have we heard this reading over the years? The names of the places that the visitors to Jerusalem came from are familiar because we have heard them before. But do we know where these places are? Some sound as if they are places on the moon! Get a biblical atlas and look up where they are and see what those areas are called today. Some will be the same today and some will have changed.

- Parthia – Iran
- Media – Saudi Arabia
- Elam – Iran
- Mesopotamia – Iraq
- Judaea – Israel
- Cappadocia – Turkey
- Pontus – Northern Turkey
- Asia
- Phrygia – Central Turkey
- Pamphylia – Southern Turkey
- Egypt
- Libya
- Cyrene – Libya
- Rome
- Crete
- Arabia

Get a map or draw a map and mark on it where these places are.

Think how long it would have taken those visitors to get from their home-lands to Jerusalem. How would they have travelled there? What routes might they have taken? Get inside the story and think what an amazing thing it was that so many people had come from so far to Jerusalem.

Another activity using the names of places mentioned in Acts 2 involves a group of people and is great fun. Maybe a youth group can practise and show the congregation how it works.

1 Get a group together. Ideally you need 16, but if you do not have that many use the biggest number that you have.

2 Give each person one of the place names from the list above.
   If there are only a few people give them two names each.

3 Ask them to practise saying their place name/s out loud.

4 Ask them to stand in a group together. One starts to say their place name quietly. Gradually the others join in with their name/s.

5 Build up to a crescendo when they are all saying their names quite loudly – all looking at each other and not understanding what is being said.

6 Slowly each one starts to say 'love one another' over and over again until they are all saying it. To start with they say it at different times so it sounds like gibberish, but gradually they come to say it all together.

7 When they are all saying it together, they start to understand each other.

8 Finally they stop speaking and just turn to each other and have a hug.

Perform this in church on Pentecost Sunday to the congregation.

Banners and altar frontals

1   Make an altar frontal or banner with the names of the places that everyone in Jerusalem came from around the edge. Add some of your own local places. Write in large decorated letters in the middle 'Love One Another'.

2   Make two banners. On one write the names of all the places that the people in Jerusalem came from around the edge. On the other write names of places in your neighbourhood around the edge, or places in the world where there is conflict. On both banners write 'Come, Holy Spirit' in the centre.

3   When Peter speaks to the visitors in Jerusalem he quotes from the prophet Joel *This is what I will do in the last days, God says: I will pour out my Spirit on everyone.* Make a banner or altar frontal to illustrate these words. Think about what colour the 'Spirit' might be. Is it different shades of blue as in water used for baptism? Or is it different shades of red and orange like the 'tongues of fire'? Maybe you can make two banners – one in blue and the other in reds!

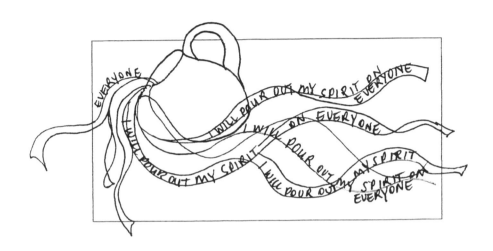

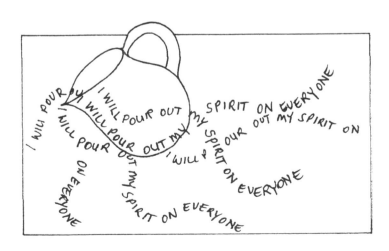

WORKSHOP ACTIVITY USING IMAGES
OF WIND AND FLAME

Look at Acts 2.2–3:

Suddenly there was a noise from the sky which sounded like a strong wind blowing, and it filled the whole house where they were sitting. Then they saw what looked like tongues of fire which spread out and touched each person there.

Think of all the different ways that you can illustrate a 'rushing wind'. You can use kites, sails, windsocks, balloons, bubbles, paper windmills, flags and leaves. All these images can be used in the workshop to make decorations for the church in preparation for the Day of Pentecost.

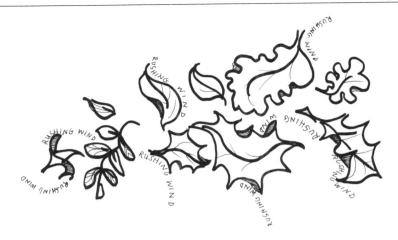

- Make some large red, yellow and orange banners in the shapes of sails. Hang them down the pillars or along the walls.

- Make wonderful, colourful paper kites to decorate the church.

- Make biscuits shaped like balloons, kites, doves or people or little cakes to share in church after the service on Sunday. (See recipes for Spicy Pentecost Biscuits and Pentecost Flame Cupcakes on pages 167–68.)

- Make small sailing boats out of empty match-boxes. Put the sails on with cocktail sticks so they look as if they are billowing. Write 'Come, Holy Spirit' on the sails.

- If you are having lunch at the work-shop, or after church on Sunday, serve baked potatoes cut in half with sails made from pieces of salami speared onto cocktail sticks!

- Make a very simple mobile of kites, balloons or sailing boats. Write 'Come, Holy Spirit' on some of them, or add some clouds and write 'Come, Holy Spirit' on the cloud shapes.

- Make paper windmills of varying sizes and colours. (See the 'How to ...' chapter.)

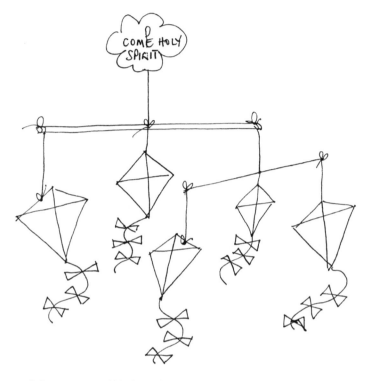

On the Day of Pentecost fill the church with balloons. If you can get helium filled balloons they will move about in the hot air currents. If you can afford it, give everyone a helium filled balloon when they arrive at church. The balloons represent the Holy Spirit. At a given moment let go of the balloons. The Holy Spirit cannot move around among us if we hold onto it – we have to 'let go and let God'. During the singing of a 'Come, Holy Spirit' song blow bubbles across the church! And finally, ask everyone to come to church wearing red, yellow or orange flame-coloured clothes!

Banners and altar frontals

1   Decorate an altar frontal with kites. Paint blue sky, clouds and sun as the background. Make the kites on separate pieces of paper. Give the kites 'tails' made with string and paper so that they hang down. Stick the kites over the sky leaving the 'tails' hanging free. Add some wire to the 'tails' so they can be fixed to look as if they are flying.

2   Decorate an altar frontal with balloons. Paint blue sky, clouds and sun as the background. Cut out balloons from brightly coloured paper and add pieces of string. Write 'Come, Holy Spirit' on some of the balloons. Stick the balloons on the sky background, letting the strings hang freely.

3   Decorate an altar frontal with people and tongues of fire. Decide how you are going to make the tongues of fire. They can be cut out, painted or printed onto the background. Draw, colour and cut out some people. Let them dance for joy! Stick the people on the background. If you want, you can add words.

4   Rushing wind. Think what wind might look like? Decorate an altar frontal with 'wind shapes'. They can be in wonderful, vibrant colours.

By making some of the shapes on some of the banners stick out over the edge you can create a feeling of movement, as if some of the images are escaping off the paper! Remember that some of these ideas can be used to decorate vestments too.

WORKSHOP ACTIVITY USING THE
GIFTS OF THE SPIRIT

Look at 1 Corinthians 12.4–11 and read about the gifts of the Spirit. Look at your church community and think about the gifts present in the community and how they are used to the glory of God. *There are different ways of serving, but the same Lord is served.* The gifts of the Spirit are wisdom, knowledge, faith, power to heal, power to work miracles, speaking God's message, being able to discern which gifts come from the Spirit and which do not, speaking in tongues and explaining what has been said. Different gifts are given to each person.

Gather a group together and have a brainstorming session to think about the many gifts that the members of the congregation may have to offer. You may like to make a specific list of possible gifts, including such gifts as providing hospitality, flower arranging, visiting the elderly, etc. (all the things that keep a parish active) and circulate copies to everyone, asking each person to think carefully about what gifts they think they might have. Here are some suggestions to help encourage people to recognize their gifts.

- **Wisdom.** People who are good at listening. This might well include older people who have wisdom from life's experiences.
- **Knowledge.** This can include teachers, lay Readers, musicians, plumbers and consultant surgeons or, indeed, anyone who is an expert in one particular field.
- **Faith.** People show their faith in many different ways. It can be through their own certainty of God being with them through hard times, as well as good. It can be because others have shown God's love by the way they behave.
- **Power to heal.** This can include, for example, doctors, nurses and physiotherapists. Or it can be people who show the power to heal by reaching out to the lonely and offering them God's love – so healing their loneliness.
- **Power to work miracles.** God works miracles all the time, through his people. It can be through the transformation of a situation by someone's actions. It can be someone or a group who have led a project that has

changed a neighbourhood. How often do we hear people say, 'It would take a miracle to change that'? It does happen.

- **Speaking God's message.** The obvious people are those who preach or lead Bible study. But it might also be the person who talks to people in the local café and shows them the love of God – or the person who runs the Mother and Toddler Group – or the Youth Worker. It might be the ordinary person at work who speaks of their faith and inspires others to discover God.
- **Being able to know which gifts come from the Spirit and which do not.** This gift is linked strongly with wisdom. A wise counsellor might be the person who can discern such things.
- **Speaking in tongues.** A surprising number of people have experience of speaking in tongues but often do not talk about it.
- **Explaining what has been said.** This, too, is a gift requiring great discernment.

Not every group will feel comfortable with these last gifts. It will depend on the traditions of the church. They are all about being able to discern the Spirit of God moving around and through us. Different gifts are given to every person – leave space for people to fill in their own gifts.

Having listed the many gifts that there are in your church, decide how you can use them in the preparation of the church for the festival of Pentecost.

Here are some ideas for activities using the gifts of the Spirit.

- Imagine all the gifts in a huge pile. The church is overflowing with people full of the gifts of the Spirit. A pile of blocks can be drawn or painted on a banner or altar frontal and one gift can be written on each block.

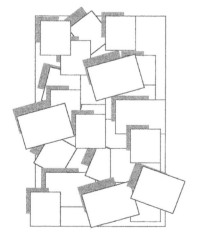

- Each person can be given a piece of paper or card the size of a brick and they can write their gift on the 'brick'. All the 'bricks' can then be put onto a background built like a wall. This can be an altar frontal or a banner. The gifts of the people are what make a vibrant living church.

- Each person is given a box to decorate at home – they then write their 'gifts' on pieces of paper which they place in the beautifully decorated boxes. During the service everyone brings their boxes of 'gifts' and places them in front of the altar. There will be a large collection of 'gift boxes', so illustrating how many gifts we all have, and how we can thank God for giving us our gifts through the power of God's Holy Spirit.

KNOWLEDGE LEADING MUSIC	HEALING LOOKING AFTER THE ELDERLY
PRAYER	
WORKING MIRACLES	HOSPITALITY
SPEAKING GOD'S MESSAGE	FAITH
HEALING DOCTOR	TEACHING ADULTS READING
PREACHING	

- Everyone can be asked to bring things that represent the gifts that they have. These can be something to do with their work life, their home life, or their church life. It can be one thing or many things. The items can be placed by the altar which can have a frontal on it with some of the words from the reading written on it:

> There are different kinds of spiritual gifts but the same Spirit gives them.
>
> There are different ways of serving, but the same Lord is served.
>
> The Spirit's presence is shown in some way in each person, for the good of all.

- Make Pentecost cards. Why should we only send cards at some festivals and not at others? Think what you would like to wish people at Pentecost and use a computer font that has movement in it:

> May you be filled with God's Holy Spirit at Pentecost
> Thank you, Lord, for N. and for his/her many gifts
> Come, Holy Spirit, and fill the heart of your precious child N. with your gifts

MAY YOU
BE
FILLED WITH
GOD'S SPIRIT
AT
PENTECOST

COME HOLY SPIRIT
& FILL THE HEART
OF YOUR PRECIOUS CHILD
MARY
WITH YOUR MANY GIFTS

THANK YOU LORD
FOR
JOHN
THANK YOU FOR
HIS MANY GIFTS

- Everyone decorates a candle with the words: *Come, Holy Spirit*. See how to write words on candles in the 'How to . . .' chapter.
- Make a cake, biscuits or small cakes to share with everyone on Sunday. The gift of hospitality is very important and is at the centre of the Christian faith. Jesus told us to share bread together. See recipes for Spicy Pentecost Biscuits and Pentecost Flame Cupcakes.

Banners and altar frontals

- Make a banner with the words describing the different gifts of the Spirit. Each gift can be written once or many times, or all the gifts can be written together. The background can be decorated with red, yellow, orange and pink hand prints and the words can be cut out and stuck over the hands. Think about the colours you are going to use. Do 'gifts' have a colour? Choose the colours carefully. Pentecost colours are vibrant reds, oranges and yellows and shocking pinks – alive, moving colours – like the Holy Spirit.

knowledge
wisdom
faith
God's message
healing
miracles

- Make a banner with the gifts written on 'flames'.

WORKSHOP ACTIVITY USING
THE FRUIT OF THE SPIRIT

Look at Galatians 5.22–26 to discover the fruit of the Spirit and use them as a theme for a workshop. The fruit of the Spirit are love, joy, peace, patience, kindness, goodness, faithfulness, humility and self-control. Think of as many different ways as possible to illustrate the fruit of the Spirit.

- Put wires up between the pillars or across whatever space you have in church. Cut out fruit shapes in coloured card. Write the same fruit of the Spirit on both sides of one fruit shape. Repeat this until you have written all the fruit of the Spirit out on different fruit shapes. Suspend them from the wires so that they sway gently in the church.

- Write the fruit of the Spirit onto pieces of paper in 'mirror writing' – see the 'How to . . .' chapter at the end of the book. Invite some people to fill the letters in with fabric wax crayons. Ask everyone to draw and colour in a large fruit on a piece of paper using fabric wax crayons. Iron the fruit and the mirror words (which will iron on the right way round!) onto a chasuble or stole. To get the crayons to be most successful it is important that people press quite hard when filling in the letters and shapes.

- Ask a group to think how they could act out the fruit of the Spirit in silence. With practice they could do the acting in front of the congregation on Sunday or in front of the other people at the workshop. The people watching have to guess which fruit of the Spirit they are acting!

- Make bunting banners using sheets of A4 paper and string. See the 'How to . . .' chapter at the back of the book. Use paper in Pentecost colours – red, yellow, orange and pink. Put one letter on each piece of paper. Decorate the letters with self-adhesive sticky spots and stars. Sticking spots and stars onto letters is a very good and easy exercise for small children. String the banners all around the church – like bunting!

- Make a big sponge cake before the workshop, using a roasting tin so that it has a large flat top. At the workshop decorate the top with fondant icing – roll out the fondant icing and cut out fruit shapes. Write the different fruit of the Spirit on each fruit with icing pens. Decorate the cake with these. Share the cake on Sunday in church with the congregation.

Banners and altar frontals

1   Make banners to hang in the church using Pentecost colours – red, yellow, orange and pink. Write the different fruit of the Spirit on the banners. You can write one fruit of the Spirit on each banner, or a selection.

2   Write one fruit of the Spirit many times on a piece of paper or cloth. This could be done using potato prints. When the background is dry, stick a symbol over the top to represent that fruit of the Spirit, eg. a dove for 'peace', hugs for 'kindness', people dancing for 'joy', a heart for 'love' and joined rings for 'faithfulness'.

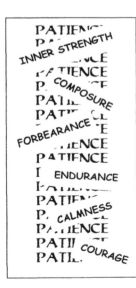

SPICY PENTECOST BISCUITS

(using doves, kites, balloons and people)

Oven temperature: 350°F, 180°C, gas mark 4

Photocopy the dove on page 170 onto some card. You can make it slightly larger. Cut several out. You can use a diamond biscuit cutter for the kite, a gingerbread man cutter for the person and a round biscuit cutter for the balloon if you have them.

Ingredients:

100g (4oz) butter or margarine
100g (4oz) caster sugar
1 egg, beaten
200g (8oz) flour
1 level teaspoon mixed spice
1 level teaspoon ground cinnamon

Method:

Grease two baking trays. Cream the butter and sugar until pale and fluffy. Add the egg a little at a time, beating after each addition. Stir in the flour, mixed spice and cinnamon and mix to a fairly firm dough. Knead lightly and roll out 0.5cm (¼ inch) thick on a floured board. Carefully place the templates on the dough and with a sharp knife cut around the shapes – or use biscuit cutters. Lift onto a greased tray and bake in the top of the oven for 15–20 minutes until firm and very lightly browned. Leave on the trays to cool for a few minutes before transferring to wire racks. The biscuits can be iced with glacé icing if you wish.
   This makes about 20 biscuits.

PENTECOST FLAME CUPCAKES

You will need 20 paper cases

Oven temperature: 375°F, 190°C, gas mark 5

Ingredients:

100g (4oz) soft margarine
100g (4oz) caster sugar
200g (8oz) self-raising flour
1 level teaspoon baking powder
1 teaspoon vanilla essence
1 egg

250g (10oz) icing sugar
125g (5oz) soft butter
red, yellow and orange food colouring
small red, yellow and orange sweets – Smarties or M&Ms are good

Method:

Cream together the margarine, sugar, vanilla essence and egg. Add the sifted flour and baking powder. Beat mixture for 2 to 3 minutes. Spoon the mixture into paper cases and place them on a baking tray. Put in the oven for 15 minutes or until golden brown and firm to the touch. Remove from the oven and place on a rack to cool.

Sieve the icing sugar into a bowl and add the soft butter. Mix together until soft and creamy. Divide the mixture into three and place in three small bowls. Add red, yellow and orange food colouring to the three bowls of icing. Spread icing onto the cooled cakes. Arrange sweets on top of the icing – making red cakes, yellow cakes and orange cakes.

This makes about 20 cakes.

Variation: Make sailing boat cakes by cutting out circles of red, yellow and orange paper. Push cocktail sticks through the paper in two places so that the 'sails' billow out. Stick into top of cakes.

PARISH ACTIVITIES FOR PENTECOST

Holy Spirit words

'Peace', 'Love' and 'Come, Holy Spirit' are all words linked to Pentecost. The Jews gathered in Jerusalem came from many different places and spoke many different languages but they all heard these words in their own language and understood them. In the weeks leading up to Pentecost challenge the congregation and those in the community to discover how to say the words in as many different languages as possible.

By discovering how to say these words in other languages, we are recognizing that we are part of the worldwide body of Christ. Asking people to go out into the community gives them an opportunity to ask their neighbours or local shopkeepers, colleagues at work or school friends to translate the Pentecost words into other tongues. Remember to ask them to record which language is being used.

Look on the Internet too. Many web sites have language translation services. Once you have all the words you can decide how you will use them.

Bunting banners

Before Pentecost Sunday make simple bunting banners using all the words and phrases you have discovered to decorate the church. This is fun and easy to do. You will need one white A4 sheet of paper for each letter, some bright marker pens, a stapler and lengths of string. The letters can either be done on a computer or by hand. Decorate them with bright colours. See the 'How to ...' chapter at the end of this book. Put all the different words and phrases that you have discovered on the bunting banners. Hang them up all round the church like bunting. Leave one blank sheet of paper between each word.

Dove chains

Using a dove template cut out lots of doves. Write all your different words on both sides of the doves. Using a sewing machine sew all the doves together on long lines. You can sew them either side by side or one on top of the other leaving a length of stitches between each one. Hang 'chains' of doves around the church.

THE HOLY SPIRIT WORD GAME

This is a game to play in church during a main service on the Day of Pentecost. Some preparation is needed beforehand. Ask a group to prepare bunting banner letters before Pentecost Sunday. (Look in the 'How to . . .' chapter at the end of the book.) You will need all the letters for the following words: Come Holy Spirit, Viens Saint Esprit, Ven Espiritu Santo, Komm Heiliger Geist, Veni Sancte Spiritus, Vieni Spirito Santo. If you have found some other translations of 'Come Holy Spirit' use them too!

When you have folded down and creased the top inch of each sheet of paper, muddle the letters of each *word* together and clip them together with a paper clip. You will then have 18 bundles of letters – each bundle making up a single word in one of the above phrases.

Just before the service begins on the morning of Pentecost place three bundles of letters, each making up a complete phrase, on each of the pews. Tie six lengths of string (or enough strings for however many translations of 'Come Holy Spirit' you have) in the church – like washing lines – long enough to hold three words each.

If you like, string the English Come Holy Spirit words up in the church before the service begins so that people see what they will have to do!

Pin a list up of the different languages (in clear view) so people know what they are looking for (Come Holy Spirit – English, Viens Saint Esprit – French, Ven Espiritu Santo – Portuguese, Komm Heiliger Geist – German, Veni Sancte Spiritus – Latin, Vieni Spirito Santo – Italian).

During the service play the game! Ask people to look at the three bundles of letters in each pew and work out which phrase they have. Ask them in what language the phrase is written. See if they can put the right words together and hook them onto one of the strings in the right order – so that there are banners. This should create movement and general mayhem!

Then ask everyone to shout out their own phrase in that language – all at once! So you have everyone shouting out 'Come Holy Spirit' in all the different languages!

FRUIT OF THE SPIRIT - A WORD SEARCH

See if you can find the nine fruit of the Spirit hidden in this word search: Love, Joy, Peace, Patience, Kindness, Goodness, Faithfulness, Gentleness and Self-Control. Answer on page 174.

F	A	I	T	H	F	U	L	N	E	S	S
B	C	X	Y	M	W	A	T	H	I	S	G
C	R	E	S	S	E	N	D	O	O	G	U
M	I	N	U	V	T	J	Q	P	L	L	I
H	E	N	S	L	Y	S	A	P	S	R	L
V	J	M	D	O	U	T	W	S	A	S	G
Y	P	Y	Z	V	I	R	E	J	O	O	T
I	O	Q	U	E	S	N	O	T	I	C	E
N	U	J	N	O	D	W	A	L	L	O	P
M	S	C	K	N	V	I	S	T	O	W	E
B	E	E	I	M	N	R	T	O	D	E	S
I	R	K	N	C	Y	U	S	B	Y	C	U
G	E	N	T	L	E	N	E	S	S	A	M
T	L	O	R	T	N	O	C	F	L	E	S
C	R	J	I	C	T	L	N	M	W	P	W

ORDINARY TIME

There are two periods of Ordinary Time in the church year. The first is a short time immediately after The Presentation of Christ in the Temple (Candlemas) until Ash Wednesday and then there is a much longer time from immediately after the Day of Pentecost until the First Sunday of Advent. This longer time covers much of the summer and autumn. Harvest Festival usually falls in this second period and we shall look at resources for this. We shall also suggest ideas for celebrating the saints whose feast days fall during Ordinary Time. The pattern we use can be applied to the celebration of any saint. In addition we shall introduce a special section addressing and giving thanks for 'All God's people in the community'.

Fruit of the Spirit – a word search – Answers

F	A	I	T	H	F	U	L	N	E	S	S
B	C	X	Y	M	W	A	T	H	I	S	G
C	R	E	S	S	E	N	D	O	O	G	U
M	I	N	U	V	T	J	Q	P	L	L	I
H	E	N	S	L	Y	S	A	P	S	R	L
V	J	M	D	O	U	T	W	S	A	S	G
Y	P	Y	Z	V	I	R	E	J	O	O	T
I	O	Q	U	E	S	N	O	T	I	C	E
N	U	J	N	O	D	W	A	L	L	O	P
M	S	C	K	M	V	I	S	T	O	W	E
B	E	E	I	M	N	R	T	O	D	E	S
I	R	K	N	C	Y	U	S	B	Y	C	U
G	E	N	T	L	E	N	E	S	S	A	M
T	L	O	R	T	N	O	C	F	L	C	S
C	R	J	I	C	T	L	N	M	W	R	W

Harvest Festival

In times gone by churches celebrating Harvest Festival would be full of flowers and vegetables from gardens and allotments. This produce would be given to those in the community in need. This is still the case in some rural parishes but, more and more, Harvest is being used as a focus for looking beyond the local community to the needs of the wider neighbourhood and, indeed, to the needs of the wider world.

In this section we look at the harvest of the world and the goods that we receive as a result of globalization. How do these goods arrive on our tables? We look at pollution issues and our dependency on water.

We look at the harvest of our selves – the harvest of what we can do and what we can offer as gifts in terms of love and time.

READINGS FOR HARVEST FESTIVAL

As there are no set readings for Harvest Festival the following are suggestions only.

Genesis 1	Creation
Exodus 16	Manna and quails
Deuteronomy 26.1–11	Firstfruits and tithes
Psalm 19	Creation and Word reveal God's greatness
Psalm 36.5–9	Fountain of life
Psalm 65.9–13	God provides abundantly
Psalm 104.10–30	God maintains creation
Psalm 126	Sowing in tears, reaping in joy
Proverbs 10.5	He who gathers crops in summer is a wise son
Isaiah 35.1–2, 5–7	Water in the wilderness, streams in the desert
Isaiah 55.10–13	Trees of the field
Song of the Three Young Men 35–65	Benedicite
Matthew 6.25–33	Do not worry about tomorrow
Matthew 9.37–38	Harvest is plentiful but the workers are few
Luke 8.5–15	Parable of the sower and the seed
Luke 12.13–21	Parable of the rich fool
Luke 12.22–34	Consider the lilies – where your treasure is

HYMNS AND SONGS FOR HARVEST

Details of these hymn books and songbooks are on pages xxi–xxiv.

Go Before Us

Take my gifts

Hymns of Glory, Songs of Praise

All you works of God
As a fire is meant for burning
God in such love for us lent us this planet
Moved by the Gospel, let us move
Sing to the Lord (Awaken the dawn)

Hymns Old and New: New Anglican Edition

All that I am
Dance and sing
Inspired by love and anger
Think of a world without any flowers

Hymns Old & New: One Church, One Faith, One Lord

Lord, you created a world full of splendour
O give thanks

Laudate

For the fruits of all creation
Thanks be to God
The heavens are telling (Canticle of the Sun)

New Start Hymns and Songs

Christian people, sing together
Creating God, we bring our song of praise
Living God, your word has called us

Lord of all life and power
Lord of all worlds
Lord, we thank you for the promise
O God of hope
Open our eyes
Praise the Lord of heaven

Sing Glory

Creation sings!
Fill your hearts with joy and gladness
God who stretched the spangled heavens
My Jesus, my Saviour
Waterfall and ocean

Songs and Prayers from Taizé

In the Lord
Laudate Dominum
Laudate omnes gentes

The Source

Beauty for brokenness (God of the poor)
Filled with compassion (For all the people who live on the earth)
One shall tell another (The wine of the kingdom)
Rejoice!

THANKSGIVING SONG

Tune: Hyfrydol 87 87 D

1 Thank you God for all creation,
   Sun and moon and stars above;
   Fertile earth and mighty ocean,
   Rushing wind and gentle dove:
   Burning flame and cooling water,

Breath of God that gives us life;
Rainbow colours painting nature,
Filling senses with delight.

2   Thank you for our friends and loved ones,
    Those with whom we shape our lives;
    Grant us peaceful joy in sharing
    Gifts your gracious love provides:
    Give us eyes to see the lonely,
    Those who should be at our side;
    Make us people kind and holy,
    That with you we may abide.

3   Thank you for your song and story,
    And the Word that leads us on;
    May we follow you more nearly,
    So to make your kingdom come:
    Give us ears to hear the weeping
    Of the outcast and the poor;
    That your people may be gathered,
    And be one for ever more.

4   Thank you God for your assurance
    Of a peace that could be ours;
    Give us hearts to act with justice,
    Let us banish fear and wars:
    Make a world where light is shining,
    And no darkness is concealed;
    Pain and loss and sorrow fading,
    Love and joy and hope revealed.

© Jan Brind

PRAYER FOR HARVEST FESTIVAL

Lord of the heavens and Lord of the earth
   Your life-giving Spirit will bring us to birth
Lord of the sea and Lord of the sky
   You created the fish and the birds that fly high
Lord of the forest and Lord of the field
   You shelter your people and make the earth yield
Lord of the dawning and Lord of the night
   You colour creation with rainbows of light
Lord of the wind and Lord of the flame
   By these signs of power we know that you came
Lord of the creature and Lord of us all
   You are the most holy, the One we adore.

BANNERS AND ALTAR FRONTALS FOR HARVEST FESTIVAL

The story of creation

Genesis 1: Think of different ways that the creation story can be illustrated and use the design either for an altar frontal or for banners. Here are some ideas.

Using 8 circles decreasing in size

1   The outer circle represents black 'earth without form and void'.

2   The second circle is black and white. God created light, and God separated the light from the dark and called the dark 'night' and the light 'day'.

3   The third circle represents the heavens and the earth.

4   The fourth circle is the earth and the sea and plants.

5   The fifth circle is sun, moon and stars.

6   The sixth circle is fish and birds.

7   The seventh circle represents wild and domestic animals and human beings.

8   The eighth circle represents God's blessing.

The story can be told using the 8 circles in the following ways:

• Illustrate the story with symbols or pictures.
• Write the words for each part of the creation in the circles.

Using a circle divided into 8 segments

The story can be told using a circle cut into 8 segments, each one representing a different day of creation:

• Illustrate the story with symbols or pictures.
• Write the words for each of the creations in each segment. Write God's blessing round the outside.

Using a strip divided into 8 sections

The story can be told in 8 sections placed side by side:

• Illustrate the story with symbols or pictures.
• Write the words for each part of the creation in the different sections.

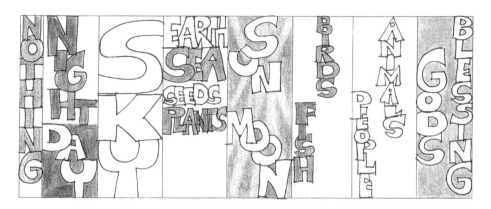

Using 8 separate banners

The story can be told using 8 separate illustrated banners that are hung separately or together around the church.

WORKSHOP ACTIVITY LOOKING AT WORLD HARVEST

Much of what we eat today is grown and harvested many thousands of miles away. We have become so used to our supermarkets supplying everything, all the year round, that we sometimes forget that this can be at great cost to someone, somewhere. Where does our food come from? There is much material here for running a mixed adult and children's workshop.

- Draw a large map of the world to pin up in church.
- Make a list of food we eat or drink on a regular basis, eg. water, coffee, tea, chocolate, sugar, rice, pasta, wheat.
- Mark on the map where your chosen foodstuffs come from.
- Find out something about the countries.
- Make posters showing the products and giving the names of the countries of origin to pin up in church.
- Plan a prayer station beside each poster and, during the service, plan to say or sing a grace by each one, eg:

  Thank you for this food we eat
  Let us not your world mistreat
  All God's people must be fed
  Sharing life and daily bread.

- Make a book of seven prayers to sell for charity – write one prayer for each product, eg:

  Thank you, God, for your gift of bananas.
  Thank you for the people of the Caribbean Islands.
  May Trade Justice organizations be successful in their campaign to ensure that we pay a fair price for bananas and that banana planta-tion workers are given a wage that reflects their work. Amen

- Make aprons and tea towels with THANK YOU! stencilled on the fabric. Sell them for charity. See 'How to . . .' chapter.

Invite a speaker from an aid organization such as Traidcraft, Christian Aid, Cafod or WaterAid to come to the service.

Banners and altar frontals

1 Make a banner or altar frontal showing a world map. In one colour show the parts of the world where there is famine or shortage of water. In another colour mark the countries where there is plenty. Note the ratio between the parts of the world where there is little and the parts of the world where there is much.

2 Make a collage of products that are unfairly traded. Turn this into a banner or altar frontal.

WORKSHOP ACTIVITY LOOKING AT CREATION AND POLLUTION

Look at Psalm 104.10–30

When you turn away, they are afraid; when you take away your breath, they die and go back to the dust from which they came. But when you give them breath, they are created; you give new life to the earth.

Think of God's wonderful creation, how precious it is, and how easily we can mess it up. When we live in God's love he 'gives new life to the earth'.

Make 2 banners

One banner can show God's wonderful creation and the other can show how we can destroy it through our greed and selfishness.

Get some information about environmental issues from lobby groups such as Greenpeace. Look on the Internet for information. Brainstorm what the sea might look like if we continue to fill it with chemicals, oil platforms, oil spills and rubbish, or if we over-fish it or use a dragnet. Plan a picture that illustrates these things. You can write on the picture *When you take your breath away they die.*

Do another picture the same size showing the sea with God's wonderful creation and how it flourishes when we look after it. Write on the picture *When you give them breath you give new life to the earth.*

Make an altar frontal divided in half

One half shows God's wonderful creation and the other shows humanity's destruction. Write 'Thank you, Lord' on one side and 'Forgive us, Lord' on the other.

Make a banner concerning local environmental issues

Look in your local phone book under 'Local Council Office'. Find the departments listed that are concerned with the environment. You might find Asbestos, Cleaning Services, Drains – Blocked, Dustbins, Environmental Health, Food Poisoning, Graffiti Removal, Infectious Diseases, Noise Complaints, Pest Control, Pollution Control, Refuse Collection, Street Cleaning, Trade Waste, Waste Disposal and Wheely Bins. Draw pictures to illustrate all these departments and then add the department names. Use these pictures to make up the banner. Write a prayer on or below the banner asking God to help us look after his wonderful world.

Reflect on how *we* can make a difference ourselves

- Make a poster to display in church showing the environmental projects there are in your area and how the congregation can get involved.
- Ask everyone in the congregation to agree to recycle as much rubbish as possible. Post a map on the church notice board showing all local recycling centres.
- Have a brainstorming session to identify where you as a congregation,

and individually, are being wasteful, e.g. by throwing away things that can be recycled, not re-using plastic bags, throwing things away when they are broken rather than mending them.

- Make some shopping bags out of scrap fabrics. Sell them in church to the members of the congregation to use when they go shopping so stopping them using plastic bags. If you have a group of people in the congregation who enjoy sewing ask them to make bags out of plain fabric. If they can make as many bags as possible before the workshop, the people who come to the workshop can decorate the bags with fabric pens or paint with the words 'Let us look after God's wonderful world' or with the name of the church. How much better to advertise our church when we go shopping rather than the supermarket!

- Ask people not to drop litter for a week. Ask everyone to go outside and clear up the litter around the church.

- Get some headlines from the papers about environmental issues: 440 whales caught and killed; oil tanker spill; global warming; fuel leaks; ozone friendly?; over-fishing, cod numbers well down; sea birds and seals covered in oil; illegal export of mahogany; elephants slaughtered for ivory.

   Use these to make a banner, chasuble or stole. Write 'Father forgive' all over the fabric with fabric pens or paints and then sew or glue felt letters over the top using some of these headlines.

PARISH ACTIVITIES FOR HARVEST

Psalm 65.9–13

You care for the land and water it; you enrich it abundantly. The streams of God are filled with water to provide the people with corn, for so you have ordained it.

As we commented at the beginning of this section on Harvest Festival our Harvest focus over the years has seen a subtle change. Instead of gathering together, and giving thanks for, quantities of fresh fruit and vegetables from our gardens which can then be offered to people in the community, we are often asked today to bring offerings of canned and dried food instead. These gifts are much appreciated by local hostels and charities as they do not perish quickly and can be stored for future need.

It is still good, though, to give thanks for what we have grown ourselves and here is an idea for celebrating Harvest slightly differently. Find out who are the keen gardeners in the parish. Well ahead of Harvest Festival invite three or four of them to come to the service and talk for a short time about their gardens and what it means to work with the soil and grow flowers or vegetables. There may be a special plant or tree that has been nurtured and has special meaning. There may be a story linked to one particular plant. Some people feel 'closer to God in a garden' and this might be a chance to share some insights. Make sure there are some photographs which can either be stuck on a notice board or, if someone has a digital camera and your church is equipped with the right technology, there can be a powerpoint presentation.

Harvest of gifts, love and time

The harvest that we celebrate does not have to be about fruit, vegetables and crops. It can be about sharing the harvest of gifts that we ourselves have been given by God. Ask people well in advance of Harvest Festival to think about the particular gifts they are blessed with, and how they can be offered for the good of others. The gifts might include baking cakes, knitting, gardening, arranging flowers, painting a picture, baby-sitting, spending time with someone who is house-bound, or taking someone shopping or on an outing. Ask people to bring samples of their 'gifts' or pledges of time to the service of Harvest Thanksgiving so they can be blessed.

Gift aid boxes

EuroAid in the UK has a scheme 'Harvest for the Hungry'. This is an annual project in September and October sending food parcels to those in need in Eastern Europe – rather like Christmas shoe boxes, but with food! Or you can sponsor a box. Look on their web site. Invite a speaker to talk about EuroAid and find out how you can help. There will be other similar schemes in other parts of the world. Look on the Internet.

Goats, donkey ploughs and eggs

Look out for projects that actively help the world's poorest people. We have looked at the scheme to 'Buy a Goat' in the chapter on Advent (see p. 38). There is also a scheme to provide developing countries with the knowledge and means to make ploughs and harnesses for donkeys. Watch out for new schemes. Look on the Internet under 'Relief Agencies'.

Water – the lifeblood of the earth

Most people are now very aware that there is an acute shortage of water in many parts of the world. Many thousands of people have no clean water to drink – or have to travel miles each day to the nearest clean water.

Ask a speaker from a charity such as WaterAid to come to the Harvest Thanksgiving to talk about the charity. Some charities provide Harvest Information Packs. Look on the Internet.

Have a discussion in church focused on water. Ask the congregation to form small groups to discuss the following issues: What would we lose if we had no water? How can we help prevent the sea from becoming increasingly polluted? Why are the rainforests so important and what action can we take to slow down their destruction? How much water do we waste in our daily living and how can we use it more sparingly?

Harvest mice

Make harvest mice to hide in the church before the Harvest Festival service. You will need a quantity of bread dough. Make small ovals of dough. Pull up two bits of the dough for ears. Place raisins in the dough for eyes. Make a tail either with dough or by using a piece of string. Bake in the oven. Hide the mice all over the church. At the end of the service the minister can invite the children present to search high and low for visiting mice!

Saints

Ordinary Time gives us plenty of opportunity to explore and celebrate some saints' days that fall at this time and often go unmarked. These people have been made into saints because they have rich and important stories to tell. Look at the lectionary and note which saints' days fall during Ordinary Time. These include St Columba of Iona, St Thomas, St Aidan of Lindisfarne, St Francis of Assisi and St Hilda of Whitby to name but a few.

READINGS FOR SAINTS

Look in a Bible for references to specific biblical saints. This list includes the set readings for All Saints Day.

Deuteronomy 32.1–4	Let my teaching fall like rain
Psalm 24.1–6	The earth is the Lord's, and everything in it
Psalm 34.1–10	Fear the Lord, you his saints
Psalm 149	Let the saints rejoice
Isaiah 6.1–8	Whom shall I send?
Isaiah 25.6–9	We trusted in the Lord and he saved us
Isaiah 42.10–12	Proclaim his praise in the islands
Daniel 7.1–3, 15–18	Daniel's dreams
Wisdom 3.1–9	Kindness and mercy to the ones he has chosen
Matthew 5.1–12	Beatitudes
Luke 6.20–31	Beatitudes
John 11.32–44	Lazarus is raised from the dead
John 14.1–7	The way, the truth and the life
Ephesians 1.11–23	Thanksgiving
1 John 3.1–3	To be called children of God
Revelation 7.9–17	The great multitude
Revelation 21.1–6a	He will wipe every tear from their eyes

HYMNS AND SONGS FOR SAINTS

Details of these hymn books and songbooks are on pages xxi–xxiv.

Common Ground

I, the Lord of sea and sky
Sing for God's glory
Spirit of God, unseen as the wind
Tree of Life

God Beyond All Names

Saints in glory

Hymns Old and New: New Anglican Edition

As Jacob with travel was weary one day
Make me a channel of your peace
O God of Bethel, by whose hand

Laudate

By all your saints still striving
For all the saints who showed your love
Into a world of darkness
Lord, who in thy perfect wisdom

Liturgical Hymns Old and New

O when the saints go marching in
Praise to God for saints and martyrs

Love from Below

From Erin's shores Columba came

New Start Hymns and Songs

Gracious God, in adoration
Overflow with joy and gladness

Sing Glory

God we praise you! God we bless you!
Light of the minds that know him
Rejoice in God's saints
Sent by the Lord am I
Through all the changing scenes of life
We are called to stand together
We are marching

BANNERS AND ALTAR FRONTALS
FOR SPECIFIC SAINTS

1   Read as much as possible about the saint's life. There are masses of books about the saints or look on the Internet.
2   Pick out and write down key words, events and phrases about the saint.
3   Cut out pieces of paper in different colours and sizes.
4   Write the different words, events and phrases on the pieces of paper. Write in various styles using different colours, or cut out newsprint. Make each one as different as possible.
5   Measure and cut out a background piece of paper of the required size. The 'How to ...' chapter shows you how to make a paper altar frontal.
6   Stick the prepared words onto the background.

ST AIDAN

BORN 600 AD

PEACEFUL

LOVE OF PRAYER

FREED SLAVES

GAVE HIS HORSE AWAY

GENTLE

31ST AUGUST

BISHOP TO KING OSWALD

ENCOURAGED WOMEN

CARED FOR THE POOR AND SICK

LINDISFARNE

SELF-RESTRAINT

BISHOP OF NORTHUMBRIA

PURITY

EDUCATION

LEARNT ENGLISH

DIED BAMBURGH 651 AD

TALKED TO PEOPLE

LABOURER

LIFELINE FOR A SAINT

A lifeline is a way to illustrate a person's journey from birth to the present day or to their death. We have drawn a lifeline for St Columba but you can use the same method for mapping out anyone's life.

A line is drawn on a sheet of paper. It can be straight, zigzagged or curved – whatever seems appropriate to the person whose life is being illustrated.

The start of the line is their birth and this can be marked by their date of birth. Significant events in their life are marked along the line using dates, words or illustrations.

The end of the line is their death or, if they are still alive, the present date. Continue the line, if you like, to show that the journey goes on into the unknown.

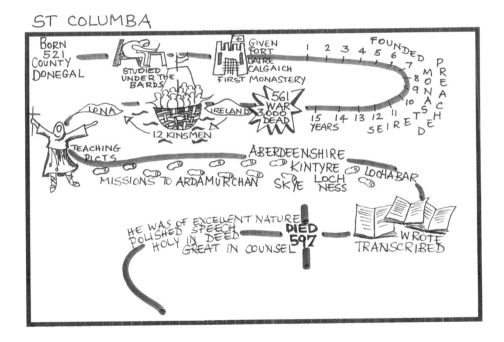

WORKSHOP TO PREPARE FOR A SAINT'S DAY

Choose a saint and organize a workshop in advance to plan the Sunday worship around his or her story. The following workshop activities can, with care, be applied to any given saint.

Workshop content

- Look up as much as you can about your chosen saint. Look on the Internet or go to a library or Diocesan Education Centre.
- Write down key events and phrases and 'sayings'.
- Draw a lifeline showing key events in the saint's life.
- Choose songs, hymns, Bible and other readings that seem to be particularly associated with your saint and with his or her character.
- Find out if there is a special prayer dedicated to your chosen saint. Make prayer cards to give away.
- Write prayers that resonate with the character of your saint.
- Make banners and altar frontals decorated with symbols or sayings from your saint.
- Act out your saint's story.
- Relate the saint's life to our lives today.
- Have a party to celebrate at the end of the workshop, and at the end of the service in church.

STOP
DOUBTING.
BELIEVE

All God's People in the Community

This chapter in the Ordinary Time section looks not only at our church congregations but also outside the church walls to people in the local community and beyond. Who are our neighbours? What do they do in their lives? How can we learn about each other? How can we draw them into our church family – or at least invite them to share hospitality with us?

We have looked at the possibilities for celebrating saints' days. Now we consider today's saints. They are all around us! They are the people who care for us and shape our lives. Obvious ones include family, friends, work colleagues, doctors, nurses, teachers and counsellors. Less obvious ones include public servants, shop workers, factory and office workers, and people who work on our land and in our parks. The list is endless. Hidden ones include those who care quietly in their own homes looking after dependent loved ones. We consider those in the local community whose work goes unrecognized and unthanked and think of ways to celebrate and affirm them in their ministry.

READINGS FOR ALL GOD'S PEOPLE
IN THE COMMUNITY

Psalm 139	Known by God
Isaiah 43.1–7	Called by name
Matthew 5.3–12	Sermon on the Mount
Matthew 5.13–16	Salt and light
Matthew 22.34–40	The greatest commandment
Matthew 23.11–12	The greatest shall be least
Luke 10.30–37	The good Samaritan
Luke 24.44–49	Witnesses
John 10.11–18	The good shepherd
John 13.34	Love one another
1 Corinthians 12.4–11	Gifts of the Spirit (See section on Pentecost)
1 Corinthians 12.12–27	The body of Christ
1 Corinthians 13.1–13	Love
James 2.14–26	Faith and deeds
1 Peter 2.4–10	Living stones
1 Peter 4.7–11	Hospitality and service

HYMNS AND SONGS FOR ALL
GOD'S PEOPLE

Details of these hymn books and songbooks are on pages xxi–xxiv.

Be Still and Know

All that I am
In love you summon
In the darkness of the still night
There is a longing

Common Ground

God to enfold you
Here in this place (Gather us in)
I come with joy
Jesus calls us here to meet him
Let us build a house (All are welcome)
We cannot own the sunlit sky (Abundant life)

Enemy of Apathy

The God of heaven is present on earth

Go Before Us

Alleluia! Raise the gospel
Christ beside us
Community of Christ
Take my gifts
Word of God

Hymns of Glory, Songs of Praise

Lord, make us servants of your peace
Lord, you have come to the seashore
The Church is wherever God's people are praising
We are marching in the light of God (Siyahamba)

Hymns Old and New: New Anglican Edition

As we are gathered
Brother, sister, let me serve you
God's Spirit is in my heart
Let there be love

Hymns Old & New: One Church, One Faith, One Lord

Father in heaven, how we love you (Blessed be the Lord God Almighty)
Go peaceful, in gentleness
God is here! As we his people
Jesus, be the centre (Be the centre)
One is the body

Laudate

Healer of our every ill
Jesus the Lord said: 'I am the bread'
O God, you search me
This is my will, my one command
We give God thanks for those who knew
You are called to tell the story

Liturgical Hymns Old and New

Longing for light (Christ, be our light!)
Lord, you give the great commission
O the word of my Lord
Praise to you, O Christ, our Saviour

Love from Below

Christ's is the world
Come, host of heaven's high dwelling place
God it was
God the creator
Take this moment
We cannot measure how you heal

New Start Hymns and Songs

Christian people, sing together
Living God, your word has called us
Lord, we thank you for the promise
Take my hands, Lord
What shall we bring

Restless Is the Heart

People of Jesus

Sing Glory

Come all you people
God, who stretched the spangled heavens
Humbly in your sight
Sent by the Lord am I
We are called to stand together
Will you come and follow me?

Songs from Taizé

In the Lord
The kingdom of God
Ubi caritas
Ubi caritas Deus ibi est

The Source

Father we adore you (Fountain of life)
Men of faith (Shout to the North)
O give thanks
One shall tell another (The wine of the kingdom)
Only by grace
Turn our hearts
We believe
We want to see Jesus lifted high

GATHERING SONG

Tune: St Columba 87 87 Irish Melody (Petrie Collection)

1   We gather in this holy space,
    where friends of Jesus find a place
    to feel God's love, and healing grace,
    in sign and symbol, prayer and praise.

2   We welcome those who now draw near,
    whose company we gladly share;
    when two or three are joined in prayer
    we know God's presence will be there.

3   Our pastors guide us day by day,
    their gentle shepherding our stay;
    as followers of Christ we pray
    to spread good news along the way.

4   No more to wander lost, instead
    by Jesus' hand we shall be led;
    his word shall be the living bread
    by which our longing souls are fed.

5   We'll sing his story, live his song,
    in fellowship we all belong;
    we'll stay a while then journey on
    renewed in spirit, blessed as one.

© Jan Brind

GATHERING AND THANKSGIVING PRAYER
FOR ALL GOD'S PEOPLE

Voice 1   For we who are gathered:
for those who feel at home in this place;
for those who feel they are on unfamiliar ground;
for all God's people
Thanks be to God.

Voice 2   For we who are gathered:
for those who already recognize God's redeeming grace;
for those who are yet to see God working in their lives;
for all God's people
Thanks be to God.

Voice 3   For we who are gathered:
for those who are surrounded by the love of family and friends;
for those who are lonely or who live on the edge;
for all God's people
Thanks be to God.

Voice 1   For we who are gathered:
for those who feel included and affirmed by society;
for those who feel excluded because of age, colour, race, sexual
orientation or poverty;
for all God's people
Thanks be to God.

Voice 2   For we who are gathered:
for those whose gifts are recognized and used for the good of all;
for those whose gifts are yet to be discovered and embraced;
for all God's people
Thanks be to God.

Voice 3   For we who are gathered:
for male and female, for young and old;
for friend and stranger;
for all God's people
Thanks be to God.

All   **For we who are gathered:**
         for our learning from, and sharing with, one another;
         for today and all that tomorrow holds;
         for all God's people
         thanks be to God. Amen

Ideas to use with this prayer.

- Give everyone a card to take away with the words 'For all God's people, thanks be to God'.
- This is the season of raking and gathering. Have a basket of dried autumn leaves. Ask each speaker to scatter a handful of leaves as the words are spoken.

WELCOME BANNERS

When someone comes to a church for the first time it is so important that they feel welcome and comfortable. Try to think what it would be like to walk through your own church door for the first time.

Often church doors are made of solid wood. There is no way of knowing what awaits you on the other side. A welcome sign on the outside of the door can make a major impression. Give information about what is available for children. Think of information that may reduce the anxiety levels for a visitor. If someone visits your home for the first time they will be welcomed at the door, shown into the room and made comfortable. Surely this should also happen in the house of God.

EVERYONE
IS
WELCOME
TO
THE
CHURCH
OF
ALL SAINTS

THIS
DOOR IS
CLOSED
TO KEEP
THE WARMTH
IN
NOT YOU OUT!
a warm welcome
awaits you on the
other side

WORKSHOP ACTIVITY USING THE
BODY HAVING MANY PARTS IMAGE

Look at 1 Corinthians 12.13–27

In the same way, all of us have been baptized into the one body by the same Spirit.

This is such a wonderful passage telling us that we cannot manage on our own. We are all as important as each other. We all need each other. Together we make up a whole, full of richness and diversity – each with precious gifts given to us by God, each full of the Holy Spirit.

Look at the passage and explore how your church or community makes up the body of Christ. We are that One Body.

The following exercises illustrate *As it is, there are many parts but one body* and *In the church God has put all in place.*

1   Prepare a large sheet of paper before the workshop. Make it big enough for a small child to lie down on with arms and legs making a star shape. (See how to make a paper altar frontal in the 'How to ...' chapter at the back of the book.) The child should be asked to lie down on his/her tummy and an adult should draw around the shape. Ask the child to spread out the fingers so each finger can be drawn round. List all the names of the people involved in the workshop on a piece of paper. Add the names of other members of the congregation. So as to make sure no one is missed off, get hold of a copy of the electoral roll. One of the workshop groups can write all these names onto the body shape. Make sure you decide which writing to use – graffiti writing might work well.

2   If someone has a digital camera ask him or her to take pictures of as many people as possible in the congregation. Print these pictures and stick them onto a body shape.

3   In the weeks running up to the workshop ask everyone in church to bring photos of themselves. Use these to stick onto the body shape.

4   Think about all the different jobs that are done by the church community. Write them down inside a large outline drawing of your church.

5   Draw an outline of your church building and fill it with the names of everyone in the congregation.

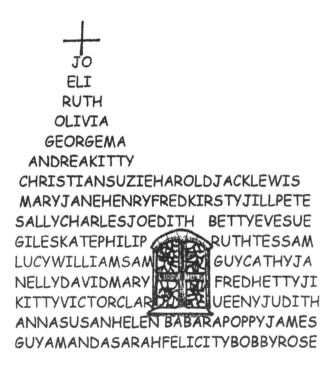

JO
ELI
RUTH
OLIVIA
GEORGEMA
ANDREAKITTY
CHRISTIANSUZIEHAROLDJACKLEWIS
MARYJANEHENRYFREDKIRSTYJILLPETE
SALLYCHARLESJOEDITH BETTYEVESUE
GILESKATEPHILIP   RUTHTESSAM
LUCYWILLIAMSAM   GUYCATHYJA
NELLYDAVIDMARY   FREDHETTYJI
KITTYVICTORCLAR   UEENYJUDITH
ANNASUSANHELEN BABARAPOPPYJAMES
GUYAMANDASARAHFELICITYBOBBYROSE

6   Collect names of the congregation, or photos, and put them all onto a background. Draw and cut out a flying dove and stick it on top. This illustrates that the Holy Spirit, symbolized by a dove, is for all people.

7   Make a chain of people. Make a concertina of paper. Draw the shape
    of the person on the top fold so that the hands and feet of the
    template touch at the side edges and cut around. DO NOT cut across
    the hands and feet. Leave them joined so they will make a chain
    of people. Get everyone to decorate one person to represent him/
    herself. Stick them all onto a background which has been cut in the
    shape of your church.

All the above ideas can be made into posters, banners, altar frontals or vestments.

There was an advertisement on the television a few years ago for a certain building society. In the advertisement there was a 3D house built out of people. They stood on each other's shoulders. As we cannot be quite as energetic as this try sculpting a church with people lying on the floor. This would be particularly good if you have a church with a balcony. When you are happy with the shape take a picture of the 'people church' from the balcony. This illustrates again *In the church God has put all in place.*

Make biscuits in the shapes of people. Write 'We are one body' on each biscuit and share them with the congregation on Sunday after church when you serve coffee.

Before the workshop make a large sponge cake in a roasting tin – so it has large flat top. Using fondant icing make lots of 'people' and place them on top of the cake.

THEMED SUNDAY WORSHIP FOR
ALL GOD'S PEOPLE

Think about the people who live in your community – but who may not attend church regularly. Organize a workshop to plan Sunday worship around a particular theme.

Are there people who may naturally fall into a specific 'group'? What sort of church experience might be appropriate? We have to remember that church can be a very challenging, and sometimes uncomfortable, place for someone who is not used to the ritual that surrounds our worship. So we must be mindful of that when planning worship for possible newcomers. Here are some ideas:

- A 'Friendship Sunday' works well when everyone in the congregation is invited to bring a friend.
- Plan a 'Music Sunday' when people are invited to tell their faith stories and choose favourite hymns.
- Teachers and children from local schools can be invited to a 'Schools Sunday' and be invited to bring artwork to decorate the church and songs and stories to share, and literature about their school to put on a display board.
- 'Celebrate the Community' Sunday can include local businesses, shopkeepers, local industry and organizations where people can bring display boards to set up in church with information about what they do.
- 'Sunday for Helpers in the Community' could include staff from local GP surgeries and the staff of local hospitals or residential homes. Special invitations could be sent to known caring organizations and 'carers' in the community.

Of course many people do not come to church these days because so much else is happening on Sundays. Sunday worship has to compete with sport and shopping. Plan a service on a weekday or on a Saturday evening.

Ask people in the congregation to visit your target 'group' well in advance. Arm them with invitations to give out and requests for pictures or symbols of their work. Ask for photos of staff members. All these things can be made into a collage to put up in church. See if there is someone from the group who would be prepared to speak about what they do in the 'talk' during the service.

Make the worship simple and meaningful. Don't make it too long. Something done simply and well is much better than something endlessly 'wordy' and only significant to those who are familiar with the liturgy. Above all make the service welcoming and enjoyable. We are, after all, gathered together to celebrate our different gifts as the body of Christ.

Hospitality is at the root of Christian faith and needs to be at the heart of our worship, so always plan a meal or a party before or after the service. This is easy to arrange if you ask each member of the congregation to bring two meals – as simple as two plates of salad. Give some guidelines about food so that everyone has more or less the same. Or have a simple bread and soup meal if you are not too sure how many people may be there.

Make sure that you have enough welcome leaflets in the church giving information about what is on offer at other times. This can include the times of services and arrangements for pastoral care, Sunday School, Mother and Toddler Groups, Mothers' Union, Men's Breakfasts, Bible Exploration Groups and so on.

Finally, this is not a fund raising exercise! It is to do with gathering up all God's people where they are, in the community, and sharing the good news together in an atmosphere of love and acceptance.

HOW TO ...

HOW TO WRITE INTERCESSIONS

What does the word 'intercession' mean? The person who leads the prayers is offering prayer to God, in the name of Jesus Christ and in the power of the Holy Spirit, on behalf of the gathered assembly. He or she is standing on hallowed ground 'interceding' between God and the people. Hence 'inter-cession' or prayer.

In a eucharistic setting the intercessions follow a suggested order:

- the Christian Church both locally and in a world context
- creation, society, the royal family and those in authority
- our families, friends and the local community
- those who are sick in body, mind or spirit
- those who have died – the communion of saints

In a Service of the Word the intercessions can be themed more specifically to the service – for example, prayers for healing, or prayers for peace and justice.

Before writing intercessions think about the response to be used. The most common one is probably 'Lord, in your mercy' with the response 'Hear our prayer'. There are no rules about this. You can make up your own response to fit the theme for the day – for example, at Christmas 'Jesus, Light of the World', with the response 'Shine in our darkness'.

When reading the intercessions speak clearly and loudly enough so that everyone can hear. Speak slowly. Allow for a short time of silence for people to offer their own prayers and thoughts to God.

Listen to a news broadcast on the morning of the service – there may be something very important to include in the intercessions.

If you are praying for individuals in the local community please make sure that those people are happy for their names to be read out! Not everyone is.

It is not necessary to go into great detail about a person's medical condition.

Be aware of the people present in the place of worship – children, those who regularly attend or visitors and be mindful of this when preparing the intercessions.

If you feel confident enough, ask the congregation at the beginning of the service if there are specific people or situations requiring inclusion in the intercessions. Make a note.

If children are to be present in a service they can be asked in advance to plan and write the prayers. Some of the most poignant and beautiful prayers can come from the hearts and minds of children.

Planning and writing intercessions is not to be taken on lightly or hurriedly. It requires time and patient listening to God who works in and through us.

As with all spoken liturgy, intercessions should not be recited but should be prayed aloud with feeling and love.

HOW TO USE COLOURS

The Church's use of colour

It is traditional in some churches for the seasons of the church year to be represented by different colours which reflect the type of season:

- Seasons of preparation and penitence are purple – Advent and Lent.
- Seasons of celebration are white – Christmas, Epiphany, Easter, some saints' days.
- Seasons involving the Holy Spirit and martyrs are red – Pentecost and the saints' days that mark those who were martyrs.
- Ordinary seasons are green – from the day after Candlemas until Ash Wednesday and from the day after the Day of Pentecost until Advent.

Understanding colour

The primary colours are red, yellow and blue.

The secondary colours are the colours made when the primary colours are mixed together:

- red and blue mixed make purple
- yellow and blue mixed makes green
- red and yellow mixed makes orange

Obviously when mixing secondary colours the more of one primary colour that is used the closer the colour will be to that colour. So you can have a yellow green or a blue green depending on the proportions of the primary colour used.

When thinking about what colours to use remember the colour wheel. It is always said that the colours which have the greatest contrast, which means those which stand out very well when placed together, which vibrate together, are those which are opposites on the colour wheel:

Red/green
Yellow/purple
Blue/orange

And a really strong contrast is achieved by using white on black or black on white.

To have a really vibrant contrast then these are the colours to put together.

If harmony is wanted, then choose colours that are from the same primary colours mixed together:

Blue/purple/red
Yellow/green/blue
Red/orange/yellow

How colours are used has an enormous impact on the decorations that are put in the church. Some of the most striking banners are those just using colour, with nothing written on them at all.

Imagine a church with pillars down each side. Banners can be hung that change from dark orange on the two back pillars through yellow to white up by the altar. Imagine how effective that might be on Easter morning. It really might look like the sunrise!

HOW TO MAKE AND HANG BANNERS

Always decide what shape the banner will be before the design is put on.

Bunting banners

You will need a supply of A4 paper. Put one letter on each piece of paper. Fold the top of each sheet of paper over about one inch and hang over a piece of string in position. Staple the paper so that it can freely slide along the string. Leave a blank piece of paper between words.

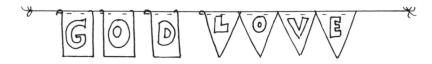

Large banners

The easiest way to hang a large banner is to make a 'tunnel' along the top by folding over the paper or material and fixing in place. To hang the banner up put a pole through the tunnel. Then either hook up both ends of the pole, or attach string/ribbon/cord to either end of the pole and suspend it from a central hook.

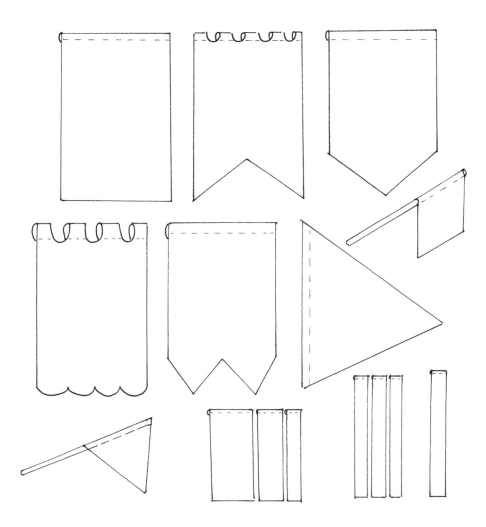

HOW TO PUT A DESIGN ONTO A BANNER

Using spray paint and stencils

There are several ways to spray paint onto a design:

- Buy an aerosol like those used for spraying cars – they come in wonderful colours. They give an excellent permanent spray but they do smell and, if they are used, it is best to use them outside wearing a face mask.
- Use pump action sprays like those used by gardeners. They are expensive if you are only going to use them once but, if you intend to use them several times, it may be worth buying some. Mix some fabric paint with water in the bottle. The more paint you use the stronger the colour will be.
- Collect spray bottles that have contained cleaning fluids. Clean them out well and put fabric paint mixed with water in them. The more paint you use the stronger the colour will be.
- Buy a diffuser in an art shop. Use with fabric paint if using fabric, or ordinary poster paints if you are using paper.
- Use a thick paintbrush, put it in the paint and flick the paint over the design.
- Use a stencil brush. This is a short stocky brush available in art and craft shops and DIY stores.

Using cut out letters or shapes

- Prepare your banner, altar frontal or vestment.
- Cut out the letters or shapes in card or stiff paper.
- Place on the background using double-sided sticky tape to keep in place, thinking carefully about how they will be positioned.
- Spray over the letters or shapes with spray paint.
- Remove the letters or shapes.

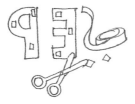

Using stencilled letters and shapes

- Prepare your banner, altar frontal or vestment.
- Take a large sheet of paper, card or plastic. Ideally it needs to be as big as the item you are making.
- Draw the letters or shapes onto the paper, card or plastic, thinking carefully about how they will be positioned.
- Using a sharp knife cut out the letters or shapes from the card so making a stencil.
- Place the stencil over the background and either spray paint or, using a stencil brush, apply the paint through the stencil onto the background fabric or paper.

Using paper

- Prepare a paper banner, altar frontal or vestment.
- Decide on your design and cut it out in paper.
- You can use plain paper, patterned paper, newspaper or magazines.
- Stick to the paper background.

Using fabric

- Prepare your fabric banner, altar frontal or vestment.
- Cut out design in fabric and hand sew onto background.

 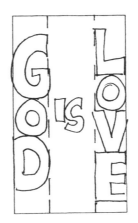 

Using potato prints or other material

It is possible to use different vegetables. Carrots make good spots and parsnips, swedes and potatoes are all good for cutting out letters. You can stick layers of card onto a base and use it to print. Use materials with different surfaces like corrugated cardboard, bubble wrap or sponge.

- Prepare a paper altar frontal, banner or vestment.
- Cut the potato (or other vegetable) in half.
- Draw the shape of the letter or pattern that you want to cut on the surface of the potato. Remember that, if you are cutting letters, you will have to draw them back to front so they print the right way round.
- Cut the shape by removing the potato around the letter, so the letter stands out.
- Dip the letter in the paint.
- Print onto the paper.
- By using this method you can repeat a letter or pattern again and again.

Collect polystyrene trays that fruit and vegetables are displayed on in supermarkets. They make great paint trays to use when printing. You can spread the paint thinly over the base and then dip the shapes before you print.

Using fabric wax crayons

It is possible to buy wax crayons that are especially made for using on fabric. The joy of these is that you can ask people to draw a design on a piece of paper that you can then transfer onto the fabric. This is done by placing the design onto the fabric and ironing the back of the paper. The heat from the iron melts the wax onto the fabric. Remember that, as with the potato prints, the design will come out as the mirror image.

- Prepare a fabric altar frontal, banner or vestment.
- Draw the design onto a piece of paper.
- Colour in the shape pressing quite hard with the crayon.
- Turn over the paper placing it onto the background fabric.
- Iron the back of the paper. This transfers the design onto the background fabric.

HOW TO MAKE A PATCHWORK BANNER

This is a wonderful way to make a banner with a large group of people. The idea is similar to a patchwork quilt. Each person makes their own 'patch' and then the whole thing is put together onto a common background. The patchwork can be made in fabric or paper. A common theme can be used to help hold the whole design together. The background, whether it is made from fabric or paper, needs to be strong enough to hold the weight of all the patches. It might help to mount the whole thing on a light wooden frame or, if paper is used, put brown tape on the back round all the edges. This will give the edges more strength. Think about how the patches will be fixed to the background. They can be either glued on or sewn. If people are not sure about sewing the patches on so that the stitches do not show, try to make the stitches big and bold as part of the design.

Fabric

- Everyone should be given a piece of fabric of the same size and weight to work on.
- The overall design can either be made by one person, or each person can make their own design.
- Decide on a common theme which everyone will work with.
- Some people might like to sew items onto their patch so the surface might be more three-dimensional. Make sure it does not become too heavy.
- As this is a wall hanging, and therefore not going to be handled, it is fine for people either to stick or sew their fabric on. If glue is to be used choose one which will not mark the fabric if it is put on in the wrong place.
- Get a group of people together to assemble the 'quilt'.

Paper

- Everyone should be given a piece of paper of the same weight to work on.
- The overall design can either be made by one person or each person can make their own design.
- Decide on a common theme which everyone will work with.
- Some people might like to stick items onto their patch so the surface might be more three-dimensional. But do not stick on anything that is too heavy.
- Get a group of people together to assemble the whole 'quilt'.

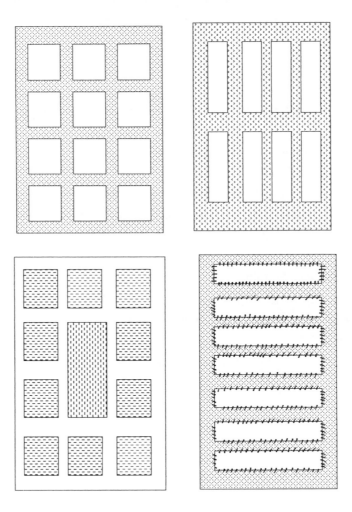

HOW TO MAKE A CHASUBLE

1 Borrow a chasuble from your minister.
2 Take your fabric and cut it in half.
3 Lay the two pieces on top of each other.

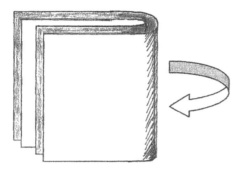

4 Fold the two pieces of fabric in half.

5 Fold the borrowed chasuble in half and place on the fabric.
6 Cut around the shape.

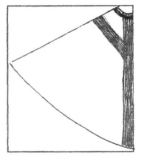

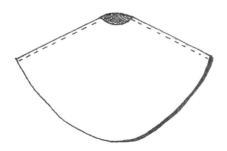

7 Open up the cut out pieces and place them together with the right sides facing. Sew along the 'shoulders'. Turn, press and sew all the raw edges round the neck and bottom.
8 Now all you have to do is put your design onto the chasuble.

HOW TO MAKE A STOLE

There are many shapes for stoles. They can vary in length and width and in the shape around the neck. For this purpose the shape will be kept as simple as possible, with the neck being shaped to fit the person the stole is being made for.

1   Decide on the width for the stole. About 4½ inches/12cm would be a common width.

2   Cut out four pieces of fabric 6½ inches/17cm wide. The length of the stole will depend on the height of the person who is going to wear it. It usually falls to about mid-shin on the person. The length will also be governed by how broad shouldered the person is, so it may well be helpful to measure the person before cutting out the fabric.

3   Pieces 1 are 2 are for the front, 3 and 4 are for the back.

4   With right sides facing place pieces 1 and 2 on top of each other. Pin and sew the neck as shown in diagram. It would be good at this stage to fit the neck on the person that the stole is being made for.

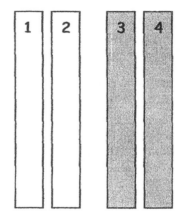

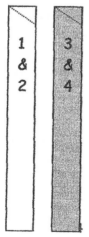

5   Repeat the same exercise with pieces 3 and 4.

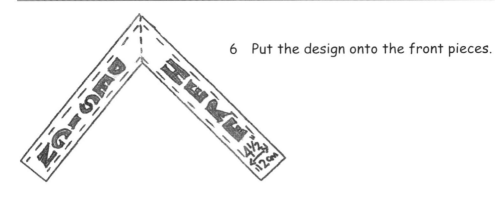

6   Put the design onto the front pieces.

7   With right sides facing place pieces 1 and 2 onto pieces 3 and 4 and pin them together making sure that the neck joins are placed together.

8   Sew up the sides of the pieces, making a long tube.

9   Turn the 'tube' inside out.

10   Press the edges with an iron.

11   Turn up the ends and stitch by hand.

HOW TO MAKE AN APRON

1 Take a rectangular piece of fabric.
2 Fold over and press all the edges.
3 Sew down the edges.
4 Decide which is the top.

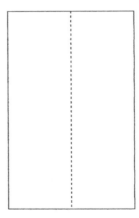

5 Fold the apron in half, lengthways, and mark the centre.

6 Unfold again and fold over the two top corners about one third towards the centre and about one third down the long sides.

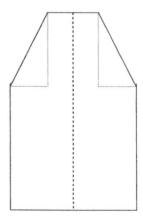

7 Press the folds and sew.

8 Make a pocket out of a rectangular piece of fabric by turning all the edges in and sewing.

9 Put design either onto the pocket or onto the apron and the pocket.

10 Sew pocket on front of apron leaving the top open.

11 Sew on a neck loop and tapes to tie the apron – these could be made from the same fabric or from white tape.

 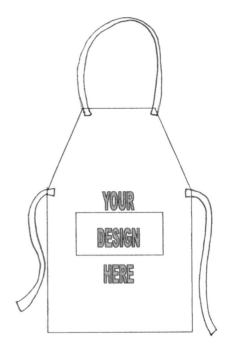

HOW TO DRAW PEOPLE

Drawing people on banners or altar frontals is sometimes difficult, but here is an easy way. Make the shapes as simple as possible. Start with the head – the size of the head will indicate the size of the person. If the figure is moving remember that the head can be tipped to one side. One of the simplest ways to draw the body is to draw the clothes, putting the sleeves and trousers or skirts in the position that the body should be in. Then add very simple hands and feet. Look at your own body to help think through how the drawing should be made. Don't get worried about detail. Banners and altar frontals are to be seen from a distance. The line drawings in the Good News Bible are a fine example of this.

HOW TO MAKE FOLDING DESIGNS

This is what you do whenever you need to make a design that is the same shape on each side.

1 Fold a piece of paper in half.
2 Draw half your design on the top half – remembering that the sheet will unfold.
3 Cut around the design and unfold and you should have a perfect shape to draw around when putting your design onto your project.

HOW TO MAKE A WINDMILL

1   The windmill shape shown can be blown up on a photocopier to any size you want.

2   Place the blown up shape over a piece/pieces of card and cut along the dotted lines.

3   Bend each cut out shape and place the outer holes over the central hole.

4   Fix all together with a large headed thumbtack.

5   Push thumbtack into stick. It is important to fix it loosely enough for the windmill to turn.

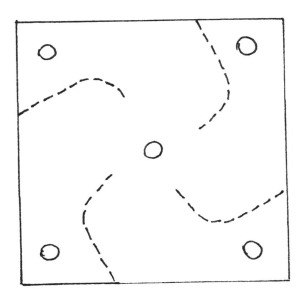

HOW TO MAKE PUPPETS

Classic glove puppets

These are very simply made
out of fabric.

1   Decide on what size
    the glove will need to
    be by drawing round the
    hands of those who will
    use them.
2   Select a fabric which is
    suitable for the character being
    made: brown and furry for a donkey,
    stripy for a shepherd, white for an angel, etc.
3   Cut out two pieces of fabric of the same shape and size.
4   Sew or glue on the face, hair, wings, ears.
5   Place the right sides together pin and sew round the edges.
6   Turn round the right way. Press.
7   Finish by adding any more details.

Glove puppets with mouths

These are a little more difficult to make.

1   Select a fabric which is suitable for the character being made: brown
    and furry for a donkey, stripy for a shepherd,
    white for an angel, etc.
2   Cut out two pieces of fabric of the same
    shape and size.

3 Fold a piece of fabric in half that is suitable for the inside of the mouth. Cut this out the same shape and size as the curved part of the main pieces.

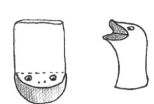

4 With right sides facing place the folded piece inside the two main pieces so that the curves are together and join the mouth pieces to each curve of the main piece.

5 Sew the sides together.

6 Turn round the right way. Press.

7 Stick on the face and any other details.

Wooden spoon puppets

These are very simple to make and use.

1 Make each spoon into one of the characters from the story.

2 Use small pieces of fabric to add 'clothes': head dresses, ears or wings.

3 Paint a face on the spoon.

Sock puppets

These are simply made out of old socks. Ask the congregation for any old clean socks that they do not want.

1 Select socks that are the right colour for the character that they will represent.
2 Make sure that the socks are not too big if a child is using them.
3 Stick or sew on any details such as a face, ears, hair.

Stick puppets

These are made by sticking simple shapes onto sticks.

1 Cut out the 'bodies' in stiff card.
2 Add faces and other details.
3 Add arms and legs either made from more card, or made from fabric.
   • When made in fabric they will swing around as the puppets are moved, giving a more animated feel to the figures.
   • If made in card fix them on loosely with butterfly clips so they move around.
4 Add a piece of wood to the back of the body taping it on well with parcel tape.

HOW TO PUT A DESIGN ONTO A CANDLE

Putting a design onto a candle is simple, but may need a little practice. Working on a rounded surface can be quite difficult when being done for the first time. One of the ways round this difficulty may be to buy square candles, but they may not be what is wanted. The bigger the candle the easier it is to put on the design – very thin ones have little surface to work on.

1   First buy the candle, bearing in mind where it is to go and what the design is to be.
2   Decide on the colours to be used – these might link in with the event being planned.
3   Work out the design to go on the candle keeping it very simple.
4   Wrap a piece of paper round the candle to see how big the design should be and how it will be positioned on the candle. Most candles will only be seen from one side so remember to design the candle with that in mind.
5   Now draw the design on the same piece of paper with a strong line.
6   Put sellotape onto the top and bottom of the design paper and stick in place on the candle.
7   With a biro or pencil go over the design and gently press the design into the candle surface.
8   Take the paper off the candle and the design should be visible on the surface.
9   With a waterproof felt pen fill in the design.
10 Using relief outliner made to use on glass, go round the outline of the design.
11 Leave to dry.

HOW TO MAKE A PAPER ALTAR FRONTAL

1   Take a roll of wallpaper – either lining paper or the reverse side of a patterned paper, the thicker the better. Do not use an embossed paper as nothing will stick to it.

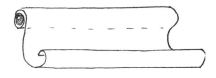

2   Measure the width of the altar and roll out the paper to match. You will need to cut two lengths to make up the height.

3   Stick the middle join together with glue and adjust the height at the middle by overlapping the two sheets of paper. Do not try to cut the paper at the bottom or top, as it is very hard to cut a straight line. Be careful not to let the glue get onto the front.

4   Turn the paper over so the back is uppermost. Stick brown parcel tape along all the edges and across the middle join – this will stop the edges tearing and strengthen the paper when it is fixed to the altar.

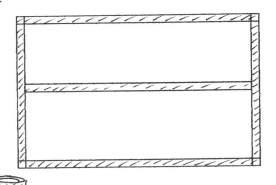

5   Think about how you are going to fix the altar frontal to the altar before you put the design on.

6   Now all you have to do is decorate the front!

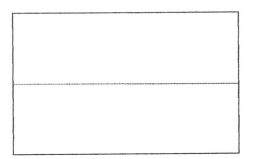

HOW TO DO SQUARE WRITING

If you want all the letters on a banner, altar frontal or poster to be of the same size, and do not have access to a computer, one of the easiest ways to achieve this is with 'square' writing.

1 Before starting, look at the space available and decide what size letters you will use. Remember when working out the size of the letters you must also allow for the spaces between words.
2 On graph paper mark out squares or rectangles of your chosen size.
3 Measure the letters out on the squares, deciding whether you will use round or square corners. (If you plan to make more than one banner using these letters, then it is worth taking more time and making them in card. They can then be used as a template again and again.)
4 If you are using letters as a 'one off' place fabric or paper behind the letter square and, holding the two tightly together, cut out.
5 If you have made a template out of card, draw round the letter before cutting out. If you do not want to mark the front of the fabric or paper with the outline, place the letter at the back, reverse it, and draw round the shape on the back. Do remember to put the letter on back to front or else when you turn the letter over everything will be in mirror writing!
6 Stick or sew your letter onto the background.

Your cut-out letter can be made from plain or patterned fabric, plain paper, wallpaper, newspaper or magazines, or you can cut out the letter shape and stick things into it – mosaic coloured paper squares, newspaper words or pictures, stamps, wrapping paper, photos of the congregation etc.

Think about the weight of the decorated letters and choose a background to stick them onto that will hold the letters and hang well.

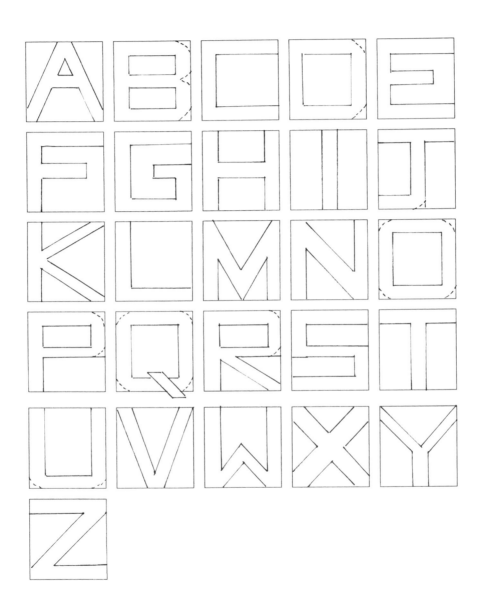

HOW TO DO GRAFFITI WRITING

For those who are not good at calligraphy, which is most of us, one of the easiest ways to write on posters, banners and altar frontals is with 'graffiti' writing.

As you drive around look at graffiti and you will notice how bold the letters are and how they stand out. Notice how the letters sometimes appear 'flat' and sometimes seem 'three-dimensional'. Look at the different designs and remember them when you come to do your own 'graffiti'.

It is important to think 'big and bold' when doing this, then the writing will show up well, and will be easily legible from a distance. Practise on scrap paper or sheets of newspaper, just to get the feel of how to do the letters.

Use a large felt pen so you get a good clear outline to the letter. Once you have practised you will find it can be done quite quickly and to great effect.

The great joy of writing like this is that you do not have to struggle to get the letters all the same size or shape, and you can sit the letters in front or behind each other which can greatly help when fitting them into a given space.

Before starting think about the space available for the writing and think about the spacing. It might help to write the middle letters of a word in the middle of the space and then you can fit the other letters either side of it.

Remember, of course, that you may have expert graffiti writers in your congregation or community. Make use of their expertise and use it constructively!

HOW TO MAKE CANDLE, SCRIBBLE AND GLITTER LETTERS

Candle letters

1   Using a white candle write the required letters onto the background paper.
2   Using a water-based paint, brush the paint across the wax letters. The wax will resist the paint and the letters will appear as if by magic!

Scribble letters

1   Cut the required letters out of card.
2   Place letters onto background paper.
3   Scribble over the letters.
4   Remove the template letters.

Glitter letters

1 With a glue stick write the letters required onto the background paper.

2 Sprinkle glitter or tiny shiny stars onto the glue letters.

HOW TO CREATE LETTERS QUICKLY

If you are unable to draw letters or cannot create them on a computer use a photocopier. If your parish does not have one you are almost sure to have access to one in a library or newsagent nearby. Here are some alphabets using different fonts. Enlarge them to the size that you need and cut them out.

ABCDEFG
HIJKLMN
OPQRST
UVWXYZ

ABCDE
FGHIJ
KLMNO
PQRSTU
VWXYZ

ABCD
EFGH
IJKL
MNOP
QRST
UVW
XYZ

ABCDEFG
HIJKLMN
OPQRST
UVWXYZ

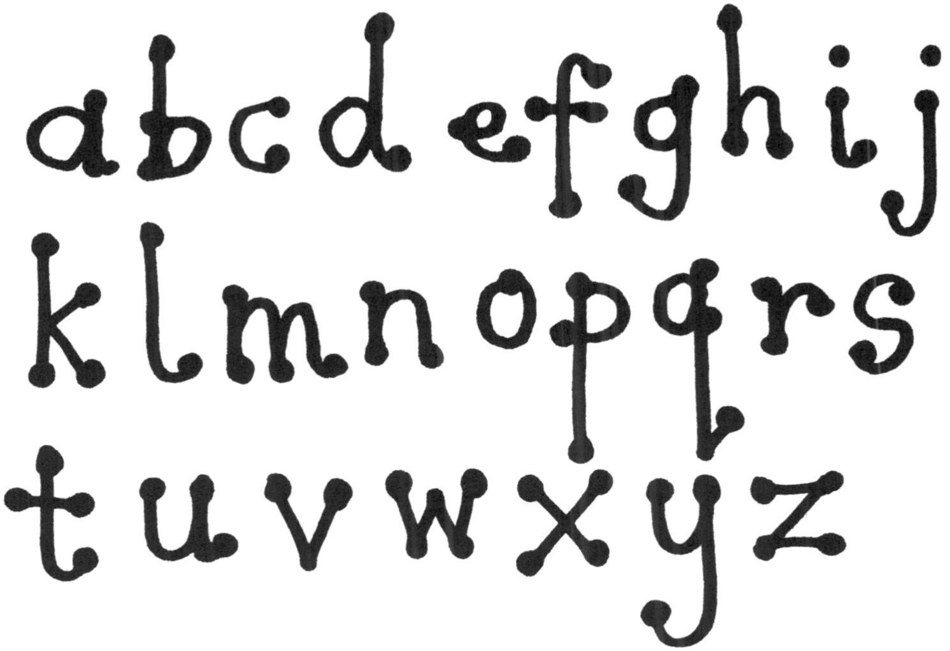

abcd ef ghij
klmn opqrs
tuvwxyz

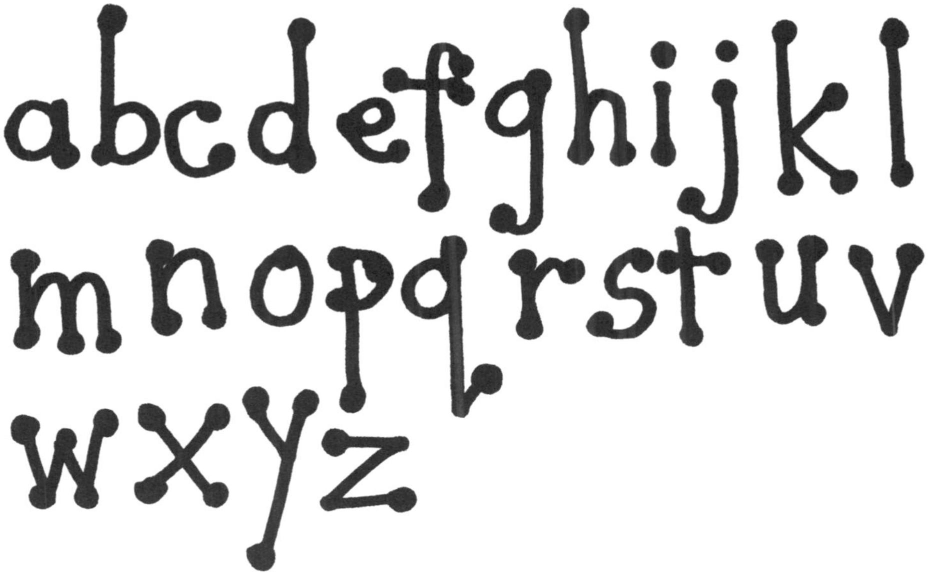

abcdefghijkl
mnopqrstuv
wxyz

ABCDEFGH
IJKLMNO
PQRSTUV
WXYZ

HOW TO FEED A MULTITUDE

The following recipes work well for a large gathering. Double or triple the quantities given so that you have plenty to go round.

CHOCOLATE BISCUIT CAKE

This recipe is quick and easy and quantities can be doubled or trebled. It is cleaner to eat in church than conventional chocolate cake!

Ingredients:

100g (4oz) butter or margarine
75g (3oz) golden syrup
25g (1oz) cocoa powder
200g (8oz) mixed sweet biscuits, crushed (use a food processor)

For the icing:
100g (4oz) plain chocolate

Method:

Grease and line a 6-inch square baking tin. Place the butter or margarine, syrup and cocoa powder in a pan and heat gently stirring all the time. When the ingredients have combined remove from the heat. Stir in the crushed biscuit crumbs. Press firmly into the prepared tin and leave to cool.

Melt the chocolate in a basin over a pan of hot water on a low heat. Remove from the heat and spread over the cake. When the chocolate has set, remove from the tin and cut into squares.

CRINKLES

Delicious ginger and cinnamon biscuits for a crowd

Oven temperature: 375°F, 190°C, gas mark 5

Ingredients:

300g (12oz) sifted plain flour
1 teaspoon salt
2 teaspoons bicarbonate of soda
½ teaspoon ground cloves
1 teaspoon ground cinnamon
1 teaspoon ground ginger
150g (6oz) soft butter
250g (10oz) brown sugar
1 egg
94g (3¾oz) black treacle
granulated sugar

Method:

Sift together the first six ingredients. Mix butter, brown sugar and egg until very creamy. Mix in black treacle, then flour mixture. Shape dough into balls the size of walnuts. (If the dough is too sticky to handle wrap in cling film and put in the fridge for a while.) Dip one side of each in granulated sugar. Place with sugared sides up on greased trays. Flatten each one slightly with a wet fork. Bake for about 12–15 minutes until done. Leave on tray for five minutes before putting on wire racks to cool.

This recipe makes about 60 biscuits. Keep in a sealed container.

FLAPJACKS

Oven temperature: 375°F, 190°C, gas mark 5

Ingredients:

200g (8oz) butter or margarine
100g (4oz) dark brown sugar
1 tablespoon golden syrup
300g (12oz) rolled oats or a mixture of flakes (or add coconut,
   sunflower seeds, a little mixed fruit, a teaspoon of ginger –
   anything you like, to the same weight)

Method:

Melt the butter or margarine, sugar and syrup. Mix with the dry ingredients. Place mixture in a baking tin lined with parchment paper. Cook for
about 20–25 minutes until golden brown. Allow to cool in the tin and then
cut into squares. Do not remove from the tin until cold.

A Blessing

GO YOUR WAY IN PEACE

Text and Music © Philip Fox 2003

This blessing was composed by Philip Fox on the island of Iona while acting as Musician in Residence at the Iona Community for a week in October 2003. It was first sung in the Abbey Church during the final act of worship that week. He has graciously given us his permission to include it in this book and we thank him. Go your way in peace.